MW00935540

INSIDE AND OUT

WOMEN'S TRUTHS, WOMEN'S STORIES

Essays from
Story Circle Network

Edited by Susan F. Schoch
Foreword by Susan Wittig Albert

A Publication of
Story Circle Network

INSIDE AND OUT: **Women's Truths, Women's Stories**
Essays from Story Circle Network
Copyright © 2017 by Story Circle Network

All rights reserved. No part of this book may be reproduced, scanned, or distributed in any printed or electronic form without permission.

Story Circle Network
www.storycircle.org

Cover image and interior design by Sherry Wachter.

Every moment happens twice: inside and outside,
and they are two different histories.

— Zadie Smith, *White Teeth* (2000)

INSIDE AND OUT
Women's Truths, Women's Stories

CONTENTS

Foreword – Susan Wittig Albert viii
Editor's Note – Susan F. Schoch x

WITNESSING
Essays from *True Words from Real Women*, 2009 1

Witness, Sandra Shackelford 3
Picnics, Cameo Victor 5
Bus Ride, Khadijah Lacina 8
If I Envy Anyone, Karen Wampold 11
A Writer Lives Here, Pat LaPointe 12
River Antics and Bicycle Diving, Rose McCorkle 15
My Gift, Shawn Essed 17
In a Motel Room, Sandra K. Heggen 20
Metamorphosis, Linda Hoye 22
Life and Death, Connie Lynn Gray 25
The Wedding Dance, Susan Weidener 28
Along for the Ride, Brit Williams 30

CONNECTING
Essays from *True Words from Real Women*, 2010 35

Between Us, Judy M. Miller 37
Making Connections, Linda Austin 38
Childbirth 1977, Karen Buley 41
Confederation Farm, Kathi Kouguell 42
The Purple Gown, Kira Janene Holt 44
Sawdust, Barbara Dee 47
Playing with Dolls, Johnett Scogin 50
Sweepstakes, Susan C. Williams 53
Trusting My Children, Trusting Myself, Margaret Stephenson 56

REMEMBERING
Essays from *True Words from Real Women*, 2011 59

Remembering August, 1959, Northern Wisconsin, Susan Flemr 61
Code Blue, Julia Atwood 63
Summer Flight, Amber Lea Starfire 66
The Watcher, Teri Heard Ralbovsky 69
The Power of Pebbles, Cathy Marie Scibelli 73
The Colors of Christmas, P. Jan Hall 75
Early Morning Sonata at Beemer's Pond, Susanna Schuerman 77

WAKING
Essays from *True Words from Real Women*, 2012 79

Waking, Andrea Savee 81
Drought and Grief, Susan J. Tweit 81
The Third Night, Stephanie Dalley 84
May I Have a Word With You? Mary Ann Parker 85
Nuances, Laura Strathman Hulka 86
Dear Momma, Bea Epstein 88
Magic Wand: The Broomstraws, Jamuna Advani 91
An Afternoon with Mr. Morgan, Helen (Len) Leatherwood 94
The Face in the Mirror, Joyce Boatright 96
Ugly Duckling to Howling Wolf, Rhonda Wiley-Jones 98

RECOGNIZING
Essays from *True Words from Real Women*, 2013 101

The Little Girl in the Photograph, Pat Bean 103
A Child's Sorrow, Kim Heikkila 106
Barbie Doll, Juliana Lightle 110
Tripping Around John's Barn, Judy Sheer Watters 110
My Daughter's Baby, Jane Louise Steig Parsons 113
The Vacation, Susan Lines 114
The Right Thing? Sheila McNaughton 116
Lucky Dog, Sallie Moffit 120

ACTING

Essays from *True Words from Real Women,* 2014 123

Wild Lavender, Linda M. Hasselstrom 125
Warrior's Pentacle, Juniper 128
Rosary Beads, Mary De Vries 130
Heart, Jeanne Guy 132
The Cat Came Back, Jude Walsh 134
Culinary Treasures, Sara Etgen-Baker 137
Not Enough, Mignon Martin 141
Invisible, Lucy Painter 143

NURTURING

Essays from *Real Women Write,* 2015 147

Warrior Mother, Lois Ann Bull 149
Fragments From My Childhood, Sipra Roy 152
Bread on the Grass, Linda C. Wisniewski 156
Cloud Formations, Lanie Tankard 158
An Elf Comes Home, Bonnie Frazier 161
Things Aren't Always What They Seem, Bonnie DeMars . 163
I Can't Breathe, Mary Jo Doig 166
An Imagined Phone Conversation, Debra Dolan 168
I Should Have Raised My Hand, Stacy Brookman 170
Car Tools Boxes, Merimée Moffitt 171
The House, Jo Virgil 173
This Leave-Taking, Sally Nielsen 175

GROWING
Essays from *Real Women Write,* 2016 179

    Table for Five, Janice Strohmeier 181
    Ordinary Days, Susan Wittig Albert 184
    Kitchen Revolution, Penelope Starr 187
    Waking Up, Mary Lee Fulkerson 190
    Becoming an Elder of the Earth, Deborah Doblado Bowers 193
    The Block Party, Maya Lazarus 196
    You Have to Be Carefully Taught, Ethel Lee-Miller 197
    Long-ago Romance, Marian McCaa Thomas 199
    Stripper, Carol Ziel 201
    Women's Wisdom: The Paper Trail, Connie Spittler 202

About the Contributors 207
About the Editors 231
About Story Circle Network:
    For Women with Stories to Tell 233
Books Published by Story Circle Network 235

Foreword

by Susan Wittig Albert

What would happen if one woman told the truth about her life?
The world would split open.
— Muriel Rukeyser

THROUGHOUT HUMAN HISTORY, it has been the stories of men that have attracted and held our attention—stories about making war and making things, about trickery and derring-do, about exploring new lands and bringing home the bacon. Around innumerable campfires and village hearths, men's stories were the stories that were told. And when men learned to write (women were latecomers to that art), theirs were the stories that were written down.

Women, naturally, appeared in these stories, often in starring roles. Eve was cast as the cause of Adam's fall, Helen as the downfall of Troy, Penelope as Ulysses' devotedly dutiful wife. But these were (and are) women's lives as told by male storytellers, for the appreciation of (largely) male audiences. So men's stories about women were accepted as true stories, and everybody was fooled.

Including women. For storytelling is persuasive, and most of us believed that we were (or ought to be) like the women in men's tales. We waited patiently at home, while men discovered new continents. We loved men, while men loved ideas. We gave birth to children while men gave birth to writing and the electric light and the airplane and the bomb.

But underneath the facade of conformable docility, beneath the appearance of a life shaped by men's stories of how women ought to think and act, there echoes a different story, a true story. My story. Your story. *Our* stories. By telling our real, true women's stories, we help to show that women's lives aren't lived as men have taught us to imagine them. We challenge and correct the myths and made-up stories about women's lives. Our stories are more than idle gossip, family chitchat, more than old wives' tales—although they are these things, too, and isn't that wonderful?

I rejoice in the stories in this collection, for they are the real, true stories of real women who write about the ordinary events of their ordinary lives. Stories about seeing with new eyes, connecting with the heart, remembering the past, reveling in the present, waking up to a new future. Stories about acting, nurturing, growing. Losing and mourning. Finding and celebrating. Life—ordinary *and* extraordinary—seen from a woman's point of view, told in a woman's voice.

But while these stories are grounded in the daily realities of individual lives, they tell us a communal story. A story about women's courage in the face of disaster, of stubborn refusal to accept the status quo, of remembering the past so vividly that it becomes present. Her story, yes—the story of the individual writer. But our stories. Our collective, communal stories.

I am delighted to note that these stories have been collected and published on the twentieth anniversary of the Story Circle Network. At SCN, we say that every woman has a hundred stories to tell, and they are all true. In their uniqueness and their commonalities, these writings exemplify the thousands of stories that have been written and shared around the circles of the Story Circle Network.

I invite you to enjoy and learn from each one.

EDITOR'S NOTE

by Susan F. Schoch

The globe moves to the magnificent hubbub
of happiness, sadness, love, laughter,
grieving, and anger, as women's words sing out,
each story separate, yet each story connected by a
mystical thread reaching back to ancient times.
— Connie Spittler

Inside and out, personally and publicly, writing about one's life is most compelling when the reader can feel both the truth and the story in it. That ineffable appeal was the basic rubric for choosing the pieces included in *Inside and Out: Women's Truths, Women's Stories.* These essays are vibrant with telling, resonant with giving voice.

And giving voice to real women's lives is the fundamental mission at Story Circle Network. Since the first volume in 2002, SCN has created fifteen annual member Anthologies, publishing a total of about 650 pieces, most of them lifewriting and poetry. This rich trove of women's writing called out for us to create a book from the bounty. To simplify the selection process, and clarify the result, we focused on lifewriting, drawing from the eight most recent issues of the Anthology, 2009–2016. It was, nonetheless, a challenge to reduce the profusion to a manageable volume. The 76 pieces included here are works that stand out.

As current editor of the Anthology, *Real Women Write: Sharing Our Stories, Sharing Our Lives,* I was honored to lead the SCN team responsible for selecting this verbal chorus: Susan Wittig Albert, Mary Jo Doig, Pat LaPointe, Jo Virgil, and Jude Walsh, all skilled authors and teachers. We had no rules; we were looking for words that called to us.

We found important stories, sweet stories, stories of tragedy, love, pain, passion, humor, and gratitude. We discovered essays that feel timeless, chronicles that recreate vanished times, and tales that every woman knows as the shared experience of being female. In stories of every age, cast in places far and near, we found lyrical language, and language that made us laugh.

After months of selection and evaluation, we eventually came to this collection. I take responsibility and pleasure in it, along with Susan Wittig Albert's anchoring and energetic creative participation. Amber Lea Starfire (2009-2010) and Mary Jo Doig (2011-2013) were editors of the Anthology during the years when it was titled *True Words from Real Women.* Their wonderful selections and editing play a large part here, as well.

Ordering the pieces was a challenge. Grouping them by publication year made sense. Alphabetical listings did not. As we read, strands of women's experience gradually appeared: Witnessing, Connecting, Remembering, Waking, Recognizing, Acting, Nurturing, Growing. The pieces sorted themselves into an irregular but flowing whole.

Inside and Out reflects the two vivid realities of women's lives—our inner and most sacred private world, and the outside world of all that teaches and needs us. With courage, each of these writing women transformed her experience into a narrative that expresses a truth we can recognize, giving voice to herself and giving us a chance to know her, the better to know all women. All of them have our great appreciation and admiration.

"*. . . each story separate, yet each story connected . . .*" These true tales, our sisters' voices, link us and can lead us forward. I am grateful for that guiding hubbub, and pleased to offer you a part of it here.

WITNESSING

Essays from
True Words from Real Women

2009

WITNESS

Sandra Shackelford

HE LOOKS SCRUFFY in his wilderness clothes—boots, faded jeans, and a winter jacket that would have kept him warm on an ice floe in the middle of Antarctica.

Downy clumps of red-grey hair sprout in frizzy clusters from his chin. He's wearing a Larry-Darrel-and-his-brother-Darryl hat with fuzzy earflaps that hang down like hound's ears. An American flag flaps at the end of the pole he waves. He brought the flag home after his discharge from the Vietnam War.

He stands among the other demonstrators gathering at the corner of East Mason and Webster Avenue. He, too, has come to bring the message of peace to all his neighbors. Tomorrow, he'll be back doing regular business, mending spines in an operating room in a hospital down the street.

His wife is here, too. She holds up a hand-made sign bearing a peace symbol she painted the night before. It's amazing that she's here at all. She died last year. Her breathing stopped in the middle of the night. A modern-day Lazarus, she was brought back by her husband before entering eternity's corridor. Now, if one stands close and listens carefully, you can hear the tick, tick, ticking of the small, life-giving machine implanted near her heart.

The demonstrators are mostly middle-aged and older.

"Honk if you love peace," one sign instructs Sunday afternoon drivers. Most do. Some throw the occasional wave or give an enthusiastic thumbs-up. Others spread their fingers in a V, a gesture once used by Richard Nixon when he made his hasty retreat from Washington, D.C.

There are, of course, the wet blankets, those who feel our public demonstration for peace-through-diplomacy is unpatriotic. I record three obscene gestures. A guy in a cowboy hat leans out of the back window of a stretch limo and shouts, "Commie pinkos! Why don't you go back where you came from?"

I wave. I wave broadly as if welcoming yet another member of a huge extended family arriving for a reunion. It's seven degrees and windy. My toothy smile is frozen in place.

I point to the horn honkers and offer a big, warm-hearted embrace. We, our small group huddled on the corner, concerned that our nation and its people will continue to breathe free, talk to each other as we wave. We move in and out of each other's space. I promise someone that next week I'll make a sign for Sunday's rally that reads, "Cop a feel for peace."

"Isn't it just something?" I nudge the woman beside me. I am celebrating the ethnic and economic mix of those gathered here in the pursuit of peace. *What a long way we've come,* I think. I'm a veteran of the Civil Rights Movement. I worked for social justice in the Mississippi Delta during the 1950s and 1960s.

"How about that?" I smile. "We just don't know who to hate anymore." Her eyes widen. She misses the irony in my comment and backs away. She stands at a safe distance next to a nun in street clothes. My mind's eye recalls all the faces of hatred I've seen over the years, those accepting bigotry and racism as the norm. Good people, really. Neighbors, labeling people they've been taught to hate: *long hairs, uppity niggers, femi-Nazis, bra burners, queers,* the *intelligentsia.* And now, there's the *L* word: *liberal.*

I smile at this rich stew, proud that I am bubbling over in the same human pot, standing united with people from every corner of the community, every walk of life, brought together by the threat of war. I stand here celebrating the fact that the kiss of peace has finally moved out of the church, its wish now extended into the street.

PICNICS

Cameo Victor

THE OLD TRUCK ALWAYS GOT STUCK in the sandy dirt roads on the way to the big lake. The guys would jump out with shovels to slide a board or a tree branch under the wheels for traction, then . . . out! Bumping down the rutted road until, suddenly, the dark green trees would open to breathtaking vast blue space, deep cobalt water as far as the eye could see, right up to the milky blue sky, punctuated at times with long dark ore boats floating on the horizon, and rocky shores heaped with tangled driftwood logs. Water so clear we could see the flashing fish and giant boulders strewn about on the bottom of the lake. Water so cold that if we dared to go in, squealing, toes, lips, and fingertips purpled like blueberries.

On some days, the waves were big boomers with foamy white caps, rearing up so we could see translucent green sheets of water pounding down on the beach and swishing reluctantly back out, trailing logs and flotsam in their wake. Bundles of writhing roots would lie tossed up on the beach, white and polished. I imagined they were the bones of monsters and dragons. Sometimes, rarely, the water would be almost smooth, undulating with shallow waves that slapped the beach lightly with a little sigh.

We scrambled, slipping and sliding down to the beach through scratchy bushes, shifting sand, rocks and ancient tree roots, clinging precariously to the high sand banks. We passed caves gouged out by giant ice floes during fierce winter storms. Snapping fires of driftwood warmed our small spot on the white sandy shore that stretched empty for miles in each direction. Rough blankets made of stitched-together fabric samples from my father's upholstery shop would be spread out. Hot dogs were roasted on freshly carved sticks. Marshmallows flamed up and turned black. The aunties and grammas brought out their homemade goodies and sat, chatting, in a circle, a blanket hung on poles to keep them out of the chill wind. My four young brothers made *vroom vroom* noises, pushing driftwood trucks through the sand.

My dad always parked as far as possible away from other folks. He liked to have the beach all to himself. With his keen eyes he could spot a rabbit or deer yards away and show it to us—a gift. He noticed everything, and pointed it out: the scent of crushed arbutus flowers, pine sap, froggy green bogs, vivid pink sunsets and shimmering northern lights, flaming orange-gold autumn leaves, fragile bird prints in wet sand, the indigo sky full of stars, the Big Dipper, the mysterious Milky Way, the hovering hawk. He took pictures of scenes and took them home to his studio to later paint. He liked to tell me stories about his trips into the deep forest when he was a boy, when he'd disappear for three or four days with a blanket roll, a knife, and his gun, always happiest in the woods. He was a shaman, teaching me to see deep into the heart of nature; I learned to love it as he did.

My playthings were rocks of all sizes and colors: slabs of slate; smooth basalt; soft, rounded, pinky-beige sandstone; and glittery red, green, white, and black patterned pebbles that clattered in the surf. Sometimes we spotted the bright flash of red-gold copper nuggets, flung up from the matrix deep under the entire peninsula.

Heads down, we walked back and forth along the shore looking for agates and other semi-precious stones in the wet at wave's edge. When we found one we'd rush to my dad and have him inspect our find. "Yep," he'd say, "That's a chip off a real dandy."

Our pockets always bulged with sandy treasures. We lugged them home and kept a jar over the kitchen sink filled with lumpy red agates in water. Investigating the beach, we mused over a fish or a seagull, bedraggled and stiff, covered with shiny black flies, until we poked it with a stick and the stink made us run away, screaming.

Later, we would climb up the sandy banks and hunt for berries to eat: bluets; sugarplums on low trees; tiny, sweet strawberries; tart, purple chokecherries. Stately thimbleberry bushes presented their ruby fruit over large green leaves. I would put a berry on my thumb, soft and clingy, where it looked like a small red wool cap. We could pick all afternoon with one tin can and the fragile berries would crush down into mush. They made wonderfully tart thimbleberry jam. We always kept an eye out for the small black bears that gorged themselves on the berries before the winter came on.

I felt compelled to draw with the treasures that nature presented on the beach. The fine, dry sand could be scraped down to a hard flat layer of wet, making a canvas for drawing with a sharp stick. Soft, red sandstone or a burnt stick could draw patterns on the flat white rocks. I liked to find polished pieces of wood in beautiful shapes and build fragile altars of driftwood and rocks adorned with seagull feathers, green moss, waxy red berries, beach flowers, and birch bark. (I still love to create altars at the beach and leave them to disappear like sand castles.)

Sometimes, lying on my stomach with the sun warm on my back, I focused on a handful of tiny grains of sand—a box of brilliant, miniature jewels, all colors, fueling my imagination until I dozed off. How sweet and safe I was, innocent of my good fortune, surrounded by cool clean air and water, trees and fruit, the fragrance of pine smoke, the sound of laughter from the adults and the sharp cries from children and seagulls.

BUS RIDE

Khadijah Lacina

THIS YEAR HAS BEEN A TIME OF CHANGE and uncertainty. A time of trying to adjust to simply not being well, always hoping that some doctor, at some point, will figure out what is wrong with me and will make it all better. A time of not knowing what the near future will hold—a return to the States, a new home here in Yemen? There are so many things in the balance, and the only thing to do is to wait and be patient.

Once or twice a week, my husband will say, "Wanna go for a ride?" And within ten minutes I have all my *hijaab* on, my good old Reeboks tied, and I am out the door. We walk, arm in arm, to the nearest large street and wait for a bus. Each route has its own signal. Move your finger in a downward spiral for Daairee, or Ring Road. Hayl is a back and forth rocking motion with your hand, and so on. If it doesn't much matter which bus you get on, simply point down, as in "Stop right here," or, as I usually end up doing, wave frantically at the bus and hope it will stop! Because this is a Muslim country, the buses are segregated; women and men do not sit side by side in the same seat unless they are married or have a familial relationship, such as mother and son or sister and brother. So at times I sit next to another woman, but I like it best when my husband and I sit side-by-side, holding hands and enjoying the ride.

Nighttime is the best time for bus riding. The streets are lit up, as are the beautiful stained glass windows in many of the buildings. People are out shopping and visiting. The restaurants and juice and tea shops are full of men, some sitting at tables sipping freshly made lime or mango juice, others crouching on the ground eating bean sandwiches and drinking tea. Men who have never met before sit at the same table and talk and laugh, and when someone new comes in they invite him to join them. Some men wear t-shirts and jeans, some wear khakis and a button-down shirt. Others wear a long *thowb* that extends below their knees, while some wear a colorful plaid wrap-around skirt called a *mahwaz* and a button-down shirt. Many of them wear business jackets, no matter what else they are wearing, as well as *jaambiyas*, the daggers that many Yemeni men wear around their waists.

Tall, regal-looking Sudaanee women, in their long, earth-toned overgarments, walk behind smiling Somali women dressed in brightly colored tie-dye scarves. Most Yemeni women wear black, but not all. Children dash across streets, or walk along between their parents, tugging on their hands and asking for sweets or a little toy or hair bauble from the merchants' carts. Tarps are spread out along many of the streets, the men selling everything from cell phones to homemade incense to slick polyester running shorts. Men and children, selling dishes, car parts, maps, tissues, water, and other assorted items, walk from car to car at the stop-lights, hawking their wares. Beggars also walk from car to car and bus to bus—sometimes a woman with a baby, sometimes a blind man led by a child, sometimes a small child alone. When they receive money, they bless the giver and move on. One can never tell who will give to them. It could be a man in a business suit, a fully covered woman with a couple of children in tow, or a group of teenage boys. Generosity is the norm. Even at the restaurants a beggar is always given some food and a hot cup of tea.

I love it when the window is open, so the cool air filters through my veil as we speed between intersections. Sometimes the driver will play Qur'aan recitation, which is beautiful and always touching. Other times they will play rowdy Arab love songs. When that happens, I pretend I am in a National Geo-graphic special, or in a movie, flying through the streets of an exotic foreign country, the sound track in the background. The Qur'aan recitation, though, is always best, as it helps me to clear my mind and keep things in perspective.

Sometimes the drivers drive crazily, and that can be scary, but it is also thrilling to be flying through the streets, careening around other vehicles and the occasional street- sweeping garbage man or bicycle cart selling homemade ice cream. More than once, when I have been sitting near the door, the woman next to me has grabbed me and pulled me closer to her, as if to keep me from falling out. The Yemenis do not have the personal space issues that we have in the West. They have no problem with sitting on the laps of complete strangers (of the same sex, of course).

Men hold hands with their male friends, and women link their arms and hold hands as well. On the buses, men sit four in a seat, their arms around each other, no space between them, and they simply don't mind. It took me a while to get used to this closeness, but I have come to enjoy the feeling of sisterhood that comes of it. This woman I don't even know grabs me and pulls me over to her to keep me safe; that is a pretty nice feeling.

These bus rides have been a blessing to me this summer, in so many ways. Being out with my husband, holding hands and joking together, feeling the speed and the wind on my face, breathing the cool night air, mixing with people. They almost always contain moments of nearly childlike delight, when I can forget the pressures and issues in the rest of my life, and just sit back, and enjoy the ride.

IF I ENVY ANYONE

Karen Wampold Levine

IF I ENVY ANYONE, IT'S THE WOMAN whose children behave when she says so, whose grown-up children consider her a fount of wisdom and consult her on life's most sticky issues: selecting a mate, disciplining children, handling finances. They call her often to tell her they love her and always remember her special days, her birthday, Valentine's Day, even Halloween. Her husband calls her twice a day and is always on time for dinner. He brings flowers and chocolates and tells her she looks just the way she did when they first met.

If she is stopped by the police for some minor traffic infraction or by the airport police for having a sealed bottle of Tabasco in her carry-on, when she explains that she was speeding because she was late for her yoga lesson or that her bottle of sauce is obviously harmless, they accept her explanation and apologize for stopping her.

The woman I envy wears clothes straight off the rack at the discount and resale shops. She never has anything altered and weighs exactly what she weighed the day she graduated from college. She never second-guesses herself about how she raised her children; because they turned out so well, they are universally admired and adored by their grandparents and their communities.

This woman whom I admire is the me I dreamed I would become when I was looking out the window, instead of paying attention in my trigonometry class—the woman of my imagination, before I realized that life is full of pitfalls and potholes, blind corners, and moral dilemmas to which none of us are immune. I still dream of her, but having had several doses of reality, understand she is nowhere but in the minds of women all over the world, we who clean up messes, mend rips in new jackets, make meals for a week from a pound of ground meat and chicken, and entertain their mothers-in-law when they come to town for a visit.

The only thing lacking in the lives of real women is appreciation and recognition. Nobel prizes are not awarded for carpooling the neighborhood kids to soccer practices and Scout camps. What keeps the real woman going is the deep, gut-intuitive knowledge that if she and all her compatriots stopped producing their products, the world would collapse within twenty-four hours.

A WRITER LIVES HERE

Pat LaPointe

LIKE MANY WOMEN OF MY GENERATION—now lodged between baby boomer and senior citizen—I grew up having my voice muted, silenced, ignored, and sometimes ridiculed: "Patty, be quiet." "Who asked you?" "What nonsense are you spewing now?" It didn't take more than ten years for me to learn to keep my words to myself.

I yearned for a diary. A pink one with a ballerina and a key like the one my friend Ann had. I could keep my key in my underwear drawer and write in my diary sitting in my closet just like she did. But when I asked for one, the answer was, "What do you have to say that you can't say to all of us?" An interesting response, considering they were the ones who silenced me.

In my teens, I found my first outlet for writing. I wrote to my boyfriend, the boy who would later become my first husband. I not only had a chance to share my thoughts, but also had my first experience of satisfaction, and dare I say pride, about what I wrote.

I also had my first experience of someone appreciating my words. He appreciated them so much that when we married, while he was in his freshman year of college, I became responsible for writing his essays, compositions, and take-home tests! No one was more surprised than I when he got A's on these assignments. I wasn't writing for me, but I *was* writing.

The children came: two, then one, then one more. Busy was an understatement. My writing came in the form of an occasional entry into a journal. It didn't have a ballerina, and I didn't need a key. The kids were too young and my husband basically didn't care what I had to say (one reason he became an ex-husband). These entries were characteristically depressing and had the tone of "woe is me." I quit writing. If I could only write about sadness and frustration, why bother? I didn't need a reminder of how miserable I felt.

At some point in my twenties, I realized that maybe I was smarter than I thought or was led to believe. I went to college and then to grad school. I finally had "permission" to write. And write I did. I longed for classes with many papers and essay tests to write. I was finally beginning to get the idea that I liked to write. I found jobs that required writing reports, introductions to books, and research papers. I was in heaven.

After I quit working, I realized that all my writing had been for others. The little girl who wanted the pink diary with the ballerina and the key was still clamoring to express herself.

I started slowly—little notes, then paragraphs, then essays. They weren't in the pink diary, but I hid them just the same. Then one day, while surfing the web, I found Story Circle Network. The universe had sent me a gift. First I was just a member, still concerned that what I had to say wasn't valuable, smart enough, clear enough, or would be ridiculed (enter the voice of Mom and Dad). I took the leap and became part of my first e-circle. I was stunned when I received responses to my first submission. No one found it silly, everyone "got" it, and no one was negative. What strange place had I entered?

Joining SCN was just the beginning. Once I started writing I couldn't stop, nor did I want to. My family still wondered what I would have to write about, but they stopped asking after three essays were published.

The other part of my writing life, the *Where I Write*, sounds a bit like Goldilocks and the Three Bears. When I first started writing, I chose an extra upstairs bedroom as my space; it was too small to hold all my books. I moved to the basement: too dark, too cold. But more importantly, I began to feel like I was hiding my writing in an "underworld." I needed to do something radical. I brought my writing to the first floor, to a sitting room right next to the front door. I decorated it in my favorite colors and covered the windows with sheer curtains. Now the light shines in on my writing and when someone enters my house, it is obvious a writer lives here.

RIVER ANTICS AND BICYCLE DIVING

Rose McCorkle

THE RIVER WAS A PLAYGROUND FOR MY FAMILY. My brother Dean, sister Rachel, and I loved to swim, play, and fish every chance we got. But we never knew when our activities would turn into adventures. One day my father was walking along a large landing on the riverbank. It had rained the week before, washing away the dirt, and many new rocks, shells, and other things had shown up on the bank. After walking around for a spell, he yelled, "Look what I found—an arrowhead! Come help me look for more." The whole family stopped swimming and joined him. We became amateur archaeologists as we scoured the area for relics.

Soon, Dean said excitedly, "I found another one!"

One by one, each of us began to uncover some piece of flint that looked like a chipping from the making of tools. I searched and searched before I squealed, "I found one, I found one!" But mine was much bigger. "What is it?"

My father took one look and explained that it was a tool used by the Indians to scrape hides. It was obvious that we were searching on top of an Indian campsite. After days of searching for relics, our activities turned back to enjoying the river.

Some days, we used our rope swing over a wide, deep area of the river. There were several knots in the rope to hold onto, and we took turns swinging over the water, yelling "Banzai!" as we let go and made cannon balls in the water. The water would splash around me, burying me in the coolness below the surface. We could swing like monkeys for hours before hunger would finally drive us home.

Other days, fishing occupied our time as we waited on the steep bank for a big catfish to take the bait. I was young and secretly had a fear that a big one would pull me in. Sometimes my dad brought home a twenty-five or thirty-pound catfish from his trotline. Since I was only a little bigger than that myself, my fear didn't seem too unfounded.

One time, as we were telling stories, watching our floats bob in the slow current, mine began to move in earnest. Then it went completely under. At the same time, my brother shouted "*Shark!*" He was thinking he would scare the bejesus out of me, and he did.

I threw the fishing pole, reel and all, into the river, sure that a Great White was about to pull me in and eat me alive. He and my sister still remind me of that today.

When we weren't at the river, we rode our bikes up and down the dirt roads and around the house until we made ruts. There were just so many times we could ride in circles before we became bored. One day, my brother cooked up a brilliant idea. He exclaimed, "Why don't we ride our bikes down the riverbank and into the water?" I stood in disbelief. My mouth was as dry as if it had been stuffed with cotton. I was only five and was scared of riding my bike down a steep bank and into the river, but I was too proud to let him know that.

Soon, my brother and sister found a spot that was relatively clear of brush and tree limbs. Down the steep bank Dean flew and went airborne till he hit the water with a huge splash! I winced in terror. I saw my brother pulling his bicycle from the river, and he looked not only unharmed, but also absolutely thrilled. Dean yelled, "Come on, you chickens!" Rachel soon followed with an expectant expression.

I held back until I knew Rachel had made it. Knowing both of them were unscathed helped build my courage, but I could feel my legs tremble as I mounted my bike. I aimed and, with my eyes shut tight, headed down the path. I felt myself go flying through the air and opened my eyes just in time to see the water as my bike and I slammed full force into the depths. The delight was immeasurable. I was overwhelmed with water and emotion. I yelled, "Who's the chicken now?" I felt two years older as I dragged my bike back up the bank for another round of bicycle diving. We did this over and over until we wore ourselves out.

We arrived home, trudging through the kitchen door, muddy, wet, and tired. Mom asked what we had been up to. Rachel hesitated before confessing, "We've been riding our bicycles down the riverbank and into the water."

Mom was obviously shaken, but she didn't yell at us. Instead, she held her breath and asked, "And you let your little sister do it, too?"

I piped up and said, "I'm not little. I dragged my bike up the riverbank just like them."

Mom nodded and answered, "What doesn't kill you makes you stronger." And then she laughed and sent us to the washtub.

MY GIFT

Shawn Essed

ON MY THIRTY-SECOND BIRTHDAY, Mom wanted to leave her bedroom. I supported her down the stairs, propped her with pillows on the old brown sofa, and covered her with blankets. Then I went back upstairs for the wheeled hospital stand, the plastic bag, and a can of liquid food. Partially dozing when I returned, she stirred a little, heaved her lids half open. "Is it time for my meds?"

"No, Mom. I was going to hook up your feeding tube."

"I hate food," she mumbled and closed her eyes again.

Since having her stomach removed the year before, eating meant cramps, diarrhea, and vomiting. But eight days ago a surgeon at the University of Maryland Hospital gave us this new way to prolong her life—a feeding tube directly to her gut. Still, the hospice nurse told me that any nutrition going into her was feeding the cancer first.

I pulled the tab from the can, poured the milky-looking liquid into the bag and hung it on the post. I let some of the "food" run down into the tube to remove air bubbles, then as gingerly as possible, I hooked the tube into the hole in Mom's side.

My husband had taken the kids shopping for my birthday gift, so we were alone in the house that morning. I opened the front windows and a breeze gently lifted the muslin curtains. Mom seemed peaceful, so I stepped out onto the back patio for a few minutes. Birds chirped in the budding maples and the sky gleamed overhead. The bulbs Mom and I had planted in the fall were in full bloom: red tulips, pink and yellow primroses, grape hyacinths. It didn't seem right, all of the blooming and chirping and gleaming.

I slid the screen door open again and returned to the living room to find Mom fidgeting a little, trying to get more comfortable.

"What is this?" Her skeletal hand fumbled with the tube.

"It's your feeding tube."

"What? Is that how I'm eating?"

There she lay, looking like an old, sick version of me. Her once Cheshire-cat smile always frowned now.

"Give me a sec, Ma," I said. No thought. No plan. Only action. I pressed the clamp down on the tube to stop the flow of liquid, softly removed it from her side, and hung it on the stand. Then I wheeled the stand out of view.

She looked at me and whispered, "Don't worry, Shawn. I'm not going to die on your birthday."

She couldn't remember how she'd been eating for the past week, but she did remember it was my birthday. I hadn't consciously worried that she'd die on my birthday. I hadn't consciously thought at all during those last few months. Perhaps that was why I dutifully hooked the tube for the liquid food to pass into the hole in her belly every day until then—so my birth and her death wouldn't mark the same day.

I knelt next to her, kissed her cheek, and smiled through my tears. "I'm not worried about that, Mom. You do what you need to do."

She closed her heavy lids and tried to smile back at me. We held hands, both of mine on both of hers.

Later that night she was so weak that my uncle had to come over to help carry her back up to bed. Two days later, much against her will, she left us.

Every birthday since then I remember her whisper, "Don't worry, Shawn. I'm not going to die on your birthday." And every year I'm so grateful that she did not.

IN A MOTEL ROOM

Sandra K. Heggen

I'M IN A MOTEL ROOM SOMEWHERE AROUND PECOS, TEXAS. I'd hoped this trip through the west Texas desert and down to Big Bend would be a sort of second honeymoon. Bud is outside in the swimming pool. I should be elated, ecstatic, but I'm uneasy, not quite depressed. He's been home on leave for over a week, out of the three weeks he has coming, and we have yet to make love. I know we've been married for over five years, but surely, even old married couples would have found reason by now. He's been spending his days out at the stable with The Major and our evenings at home feel strained and quiet as we sit in separate chairs to watch television. Something is obviously amiss, but I don't know what or how to address it.

Bud comes in through the sliding glass door and, for a split second, he hesitates, and all I can see is his rangy silhouette against the brilliance of the Texas desert light and the still, blue water of the pool. I'd like to think his hesitation is because he got a glimpse of me in my white chiffon gown and negligee, but it could as well be that he is simply blinded by coming from the glare outside into the dark room. I'll never know.

He heads toward the bathroom without a word. I don't know exactly what I expected after carefully donning my nightwear and perfume, but it wasn't this sense of dismissal. My heart drops into the hollow shell I've immediately become, and I drop my hopeful gaze. My eyes are suddenly hot and dry, and I can't swallow the lump in my throat or all the fiery anguish will come pouring out.

I sit on the edge of the bed, a pale statue in flowing sheer robes. I'm not thinking, just lost and drowning in pain. If I were thinking, I'd be asking myself what's wrong with me (with me, mind you, not him) and wondering what I did to cause him to become so icy. He's been gone for nearly a year and, while his letters lately haven't been as full of longing and suggestive phrases, and my phone calls to him never seem to reach him in his barracks room, I find all sorts of reasons. I can't call them excuses. I might have to face what I don't want to know, don't even want to vaguely consider. So I don't.

Finally, he comes out of the bathroom, his dark hair still damp and glistening, his beard stubble already thick enough to nearly conceal his lower face. He always grows a beard when he's on leave, because he can in such a short time, and because it helps him to feel as far as possible from the army discipline that a clean-shaven face forces him to remember. He still hasn't spoken but he's coming toward me and my heart lifts in hope as I look up into his dear, but expressionless, face. He pushes me back onto the bed, not harshly, but not carefully either, not like someone who doesn't want to hurt something precious.

He carefully separates the edges of my negligee and pulls up my gown, helping me lift my hips to ensure that it goes all the way to my waist. Still not a word has he spoken. It's finally going to happen. We're going to make love! My hands roam over his slim body as he positions himself above me and slowly lowers his weight with very little foreplay. He doesn't really look at me. He doesn't kiss me, either. I wonder about that. And then his breath comes fast and so does mine, as I rise to meet him. It's done.

My heart breaks, though I don't quite realize it yet. All I know is that now I understand the difference between making love and having sex, and it's not something I ever wanted to know. He rolls off me, pulls the sheets down on the other side of the bed to slip between them and soon is snoring, his back toward me. I haven't yet moved, trying to process what just happened and unable or, rather, unwilling. I finally sit up, remove the filmy robes that I'd hoped would entice him to love me, and slip between the sheets on my side.

As I lie there watching the late desert sunset quickly turn to night, the lump is back in my throat, and I can feel a hot tear course down my cheek to become icy in the chill, air-conditioned, false atmosphere of an impersonal motel room.

METAMORPHOSIS

Linda Hoye

I KNEW THERE WAS A PROBLEM before the X-ray confirmed it. Like most sixteen-year-old girls, I wanted to fit in and look the same as my friends. But I had known for some time that something was different about the way that my body was changing. It started gradually, with my clothes not quite fitting the same. In time, I noticed a visible change in the height of my shoulders and hips, and realized that one side of my waist curved in while the other stayed almost straight. I began wearing over-sized shirts to hide the asymmetry, which allowed me to keep these odd changes secret for some time. When a routine visit to the doctor prompted an X-ray of my torso, however, my secret was out.

I was referred to an orthopedic surgeon in Vancouver, BC, a four-hour drive from our home. A trip to the city was generally reason for excitement, but my enthusiasm rapidly waned as I sat in Dr. Tredwell's office with my parents. We watched as he drew lines on my X-ray and calculated the degree to which my spine was curved. He explained that the condition was called idiopathic scoliosis, which I later learned simply means a curvature of the spine of unknown origin. Dr. Tredwell recommended surgery. He wanted to insert a Harrington rod in my spine, since the curve would continue to worsen without treatment. After surgery, I would be wrapped in a full body cast to protect my spine during the many months of healing to follow. By the time we left the surgeon's office, we had set a date for the operation. I was astonished at how quickly my life had changed.

A few months later, we traveled back to Vancouver, where I was admitted to a hospital and prepared for surgery. Over the next two weeks, I spent most of my days in bed attached to pulleys and weights that stretched my back. My hips ached from the constant pull of the traction. To make matters worse, my parents had to return to work, and I was left alone. I always was a shy girl, but I forced myself to reach out to others on the ward and make new friends.

Following the surgery, I awoke on a narrow bed called a Stryker frame—a stretcher just wide enough for my body, with armrest attachments on each side. The stretcher was attached to a frame in a way that allowed it to be rotated 180 degrees. Every few hours, the nurses would place a second stretcher on top of me, place my arms by my side, and strap me into the contraption. Then, in one swift movement, they would flip me so I was staring down at the floor or up at the ceiling.

Forced to remain flat on my back or stomach, only able to move my arms, I had to learn new ways of doing everyday tasks. One of my biggest challenges was learning to eat a meal while lying flat on my back. The nurses adjusted a standing mirror beside my bed, allowing me to see the reflection of a plate of food placed upon my chest. I got to be pretty good at using the mirror to pick up larger pieces of food, but I was never happy to see peas on my plate.

I also learned to rely more on my imagination. Unable to lift my head or rise from my prone position, I began visualizing television programs while listening with an earphone, and I became fairly good at imagining faces as I talked with new nurses I couldn't see.

After three weeks in the Stryker frame, getting flipped every two hours, my back finally healed enough to allow the doctor to apply my full body cast and move me to a regular hospital bed. I still was unable to sit up or get out of bed. Yet it was the first step toward going home, and I was delighted.

When the cast had dried, I was driven home in an ambulance. I felt a little bit like a celebrity as the ambulance pulled into our driveway and some neighbors came out to knock on the window to greet me.

I was confined to bed over the next four months and had no choice but to allow others to care for me. It was a nightmare for a sixteen-year-old girl to deal with the loss of her independence. Even my personal toiletry habits were no longer private. I was forced to deal with the indignity of having someone else care for me in that way.

In order not to fall behind in my schoolwork, I had enrolled in correspondence classes. One of the unexpected benefits was the ability to take writing and literature classes not offered at my school. I spent many lonely days while my parents were at work and my sister was at school, working on my assignments and nourishing my passion for writing.

A lighter walking cast, which I wore for two months, eventually replaced the heavy body cast. No longer confined to bed,

I quickly caught up with my friends and moved back into the social circle I missed so much.

When the time came to emerge from my plaster cocoon, I was pleased to find a body that I could learn to love. Some of the spine curvature would always remain, but I was thankful for the obvious improvement. Less evident, though just as real, were the changes I found in my character. During my long recuperation period, I relied on a level of self-sufficiency and inner strength that I hadn't known I possessed. This was my true metamorphosis, from a self-conscious child to a young woman confident in her ability to survive.

LIFE AND DEATH

Connie Lynn Gray

"WHAT DO YOU THINK of a person ending their own life?" Andrew asked in a quiet voice.

What he meant and couldn't ask was, "Would you support me if I gave up my fight against AIDS? Shouldn't my family remember me as I lived, not as I lay dying, drowning in my own fluids with a look of terror on my face? I know you are my nurse and are supposed to help me live, but if I needed your help, would you help me die?"

All those things were what he meant and could not ask. My reply was equally veiled. "I believe a person has the right to decide how to live … and how to die."

Looking into his tired blue eyes, I knew Andrew was serious. Twice a week I visited him and his partner, Juan. Andrew, the healthier of the two, had purchased private health and disability insurance before there was a test for HIV. Juan's care waxed and waned with the availability of county assistance funds.

Since I lived closer to Andrew than the other nurses, I would answer his page even when I wasn't on call. Antibiotics, pumps, central line dressing changes, and lab draws were the foundation of a growing friendship.

Juan's family thought he had cancer. It was easy to keep them insulated from the truth as they were uneducated and didn't speak English. His mother came up from Mexico and didn't understand medical terms or recognize the names of HIV/AIDS medications.

"He get better?" She quizzed me on a visit after another hospitalization.

"He looks better," I replied, giving her my Nancy Nurse fake smile. She smiled broadly in her own blissful ignorance, wiped his brow with a wet washcloth and patted his arm. Juan looked at me gratefully and, in his weakened state, mouthed his thanks.

Another week passed, and Juan and Andrew were both hospitalized. Juan worsened, and although Andrew rallied, he remained hospitalized to be near Juan. Juan's family surrounded his bed as he struggled against death and eventually drowned in pneumonia.

Andrew's mom swooped in from some northern state. Since Juan had died, there was nothing holding Andrew in Texas and she declared her son would move back home. His brother would give up his room and Andrew would rejoin his family for whatever time he had left.

There were a few more visits with carefully worded questions from Andrew. What would happen if someone took . . . too much insulin . . . or too many sleeping pills? How many are too many? How would one dispose of the evidence? What would happen? We spoke in guarded words and cryptic messages.

Then, as the move back north became more imminent, Andrew called and casually asked, "Where are the large syringes that I used when I was on TPN? I thought Juan placed the leftover ones in my long cabinet, but I just can't get down to look for them."

"You know," I just as casually replied, "I think I did see them in the cabinet. I'll drop by."

When I arrived, Andrew was swaddled with blankets in his favorite chair—one more futile effort to warm his thin frame. Andrew's mom and attorney were seated, one on each side of Andrew, talking over him as if he were invisible. The conversation concerned transportation home, moving the furniture, and the sale of the house. Andrew's blue eyes caught mine. He leaned back in the chair, smiled weakly, and shrugged his shoulders.

"I'm going to check your supplies," I said as I stepped into the bedroom. I can still see his room, windows open, the curtains billowing, fresh air diluting the illness in the room. The large syringes were on the bottom shelf in the back of the long cabinet. I took one, attached a large bore needle, and placed it on the bedside table next to the neatly arranged full bottles of sleeping pills and a vial of insulin. A needle box was on the floor next to the bed.

Stepping back into the living room, I said, "Okay, I'm leaving. Let me know if you need anything."

Andrew raised his head, smiled, and softly said, "Bye." His mother and attorney merely nodded as I showed myself out.

The following morning was a Saturday, and I was at the YMCA with my kids when I was paged with the simple message, "Call Andrew's mom."

I called from the pay phone at the YMCA. When Andrew's mom picked up, she choked out the words, "He's gone."

I moaned and leaned on the cinder block wall next to the payphone. Damn. This was real, it wasn't a concept, it wasn't a what-if. This was real. I guess I thought he would be so afraid of death that he wouldn't take action.

Tears flowed, and as I sobbed, I told his mom I would come over as soon as possible. After dropping my kids off at home, I raced to Andrew's.

The funeral home was leaving with Andrew's body. His mom repeatedly said, "I just hope he didn't suffer." While she made calls, I went to his bedroom. Pill bottles were still lined up neatly on the bedside table, empty. There was the needle box on the floor. Peering in, I saw the solitary syringe and empty insulin vial. As I left, I gave his mom another hug and honestly said that Andrew did not suffer, not at all. Andrew just went to sleep and simply did not wake up.

Andrew was going to die. Twenty years ago there was no treatment that could have saved him. He merely chose the least painful way of leaving this world. Andrew decided how he lived, and he decided, with great courage, how he would die.

I think of Andrew often, and always when I have my windows open and the curtains billow.

THE WEDDING DANCE

Susan Weidener

OUR WEDDING RECEPTION WAS HELD at an old Victorian-style mansion with wrought-iron gates along Philadelphia's Main Line. It was overcast, and all day I watched the sky, hoping the sun would break through the clouds. But it never did. The rhododendron's mauve blossoms in the outside courtyard of the house were beautiful, but the day was cool and dreary.

John and I stood with my parents and greeted our small circle of family and friends. No one was there from John's family, of course. His mother had seen to that.

"They're playing our song," John said, holding out his hand to me as we went indoors for our first dance as husband and wife.

He held me close, his hand cupping mine against his chest as we danced to "As Time Goes By." *Casablanca* was John's favorite movie and this, of course, was the movie's theme song.

John was handsome in an off-white tuxedo that complemented his dark good looks. My slinky white wedding dress clung to my body like the love I felt all over me for him. Our gold wedding rings gleamed as we held hands and moved in time to the music.

"I can't wait to get you alone," my husband whispered in my ear. "Here's looking at you, kid," he said. He could recite by heart the entire final farewell scene at the airport between Bogie and Bergman. He was a great imitator and even had Bogart's accent down pat. "If that plane leaves the ground and you're not on it, you'll regret it. Maybe not today. Maybe not tomorrow. But soon and for the rest of your life."

John loved the tragedy and the romance of the story. He loved Bogie's heroism in letting the woman he loved go because it was the right and honorable thing to do. How could we have known that those final tragic moments of two lovers saying goodbye forever at the close of *Casablanca* would come our way less than seventeen years after that dance at our wedding? And would it have changed anything if we *had* known? I had taken the vows, "in sickness and in health," not realizing how fraught with meaning they would be.

Toward the end of what turned out to be a seven-year battle with cancer, John took much of the burden from me with his decision to go off dialysis. The cancer had continued to invade his body and his kidneys shut down. The doctor explained that we were "one of the lucky ones" because we could rob the disease of its worst ravages by John simply going off dialysis.

One thing I can say is that watching my husband die did not make me feel like "one of the lucky ones."

"I've put you through enough these last seven years," John said. He was Bogie on the foggy runway of that airport in *Casablanca*.

Sometimes I danced with John again in my dreams. I felt the warmth of his body, saw the look in his eyes as he slowly began making love to me.

"Please don't go," I implored as the dream began to fade. But he would leave anyway, disappearing up a winding staircase. I would wake up in my bedroom with the same flowered wallpaper that had been there when he was alive, only now the room was laden with the heavy fragrance of grief.

"No doubt you and I had a special love," I wrote in my notebook. "I knew it would be this bad. How could I replace you— you who loved me so? I will always love you, my darling John."

The man I loved, the father of my children, was gone. I had been cheated out of something that I had yearned for all my life and then found, only to lose it again in a heartbeat.

ALONG FOR THE RIDE

Brit Williams

WE SIT ON OUR HAND-ME-DOWN COUCH contemplating what to do with our first wedding anniversary money. My hopes are set on a new couch, something sophisticated and cozy that would spruce the place up a bit. But just as I am about to suggest that the plaid hide-a-bed we are sitting on is in desperate need of replacement, Spence gives me the puppy dog eyes and comes out with it.

"You might think I'm crazy," he says, "but let's use the money to get bikes. I want us to go mountain biking together."

Mountain biking? Yuck. My decorating dreams dwindle.

Looking over at my husband, my mother's motto comes to mind: *Just go along for the ride.* I force myself to be a good sport and not groan out loud.

"Okay," I say, looking into his pale blue eyes and smiling, a reassurance to us both that I am still the fun wife he married last year. And so I watch $800 drain out of our savings account with zero expectations, trying not to compare our plaid sleeper sofa with the leather couch I just saw at the Pottery Barn outlet for forty percent off.

Despite the fact that his mother hounded me about getting some "decent furniture" on her last visit, Spence continues to remind me, "Who cares what other people think!" I trusted him as we broke conventions planning our wedding, and I want to trust him now.

A veteran behind the handlebars, Spence spends hours in the garage assembling and tweaking our new red Ibex bikes to perfection. The dreaded moment finally arrives and we head to the park for my first lesson. I expect him to get frustrated with me, as Dad used to on our sailing trips. I called them "Un-Joy Rides" because whether or not the breeze was working for him, the beer would, and sooner or later, the highly tedious pastime would require some patience. Dad would blow his cool right in the middle of the Intercoastal waterway and blame the six-year-old across from him for the whole thing going wrong.

I still fear that Spencer will lose his temper or give up on me when I require a little patience. He is nothing like my father, yet the old adage that most women marry men like their fathers still haunts me. Have his true colors yet to shine?

We take it easy at first. This is not the Mongoose I grew up riding. Replaying the lesson Spencer gave me in the garage before we left, I attempt the balancing act of remembering gears and pedaling all at once.

"So which hand is the front brake?" I ask.

"Remember, be right back," he exaggerates. "Then you won't forget left is front."

I change gears to increase resistance and squeeze my left hand. Wrong. The front brake almost shoots me over my handlebars. This is worse than piano lessons. Or sailing. This time I do groan out load.

"Ugh," I grunt, slamming my muddy cleat into the pedal clip. Looking down at my dirt-caked legs, I imagine them cleanly shaven, resting leisurely on some fine Ethan Allen leather, supporting me as I read the afternoon away.

"Here," he says, clipping out with ease and walking over to assist me. "Try this." His extra dose of calm evens us out. We stop under the blistering sun and he gives me another ten-minute remedial session as he does each time my frustration level rises. Patiently demonstrating what he's already shown me a hundred times, he tosses in some encouragement with each corrective measure. I see elements of my husband that could never surface sitting on a fancy couch, even the Lancaster Leather sofa from Restoration Hardware, the Rolls Royce of couches.

"Yeah, but doesn't it seem like the trouble outweighs the fun?" I say. Sweat drips into my eyes, clouding my vision. Spence looks like an angel.

"No," he says, looking at me like I miss this whole point.

It must be a guy thing. I run my cleat through the dirt as he walks over to wipe the sweat beads from under my eyes with his thumb. Lifting my chin, he says, "Because I get to be out here with you."

I sink onto my unforgiving seat. This man amazes me.

"Honey, you're doing great," he says, looking upon me proudly. Spence leans in to give me a perspired kiss, a silent reminder that my marriage is not an appalling adage. I did not marry my father after all. Not even remotely.

I have someone who will teach me and watch me learn, a guide who will build me up until I'm ready to go without training wheels. Someone who doesn't shy away from difficulty. And he doesn't just bring me along, he teaches me how to ride—even if it takes all day.

Pulling over under a welcoming tree, we suck water out of our Camelbaks like nursing babies. Our sticky faces meet for another unconditional kiss and I concede to myself that this is worth it; no couch on interest loan feels this good.

"I," he says, chasing down his breath, "love you."

Peering into his grimy face, I want to say, "I know." Sure, he adores me when I'm the fun-loving wife he took at the altar last year, but this sweaty man before me knows I get easily flustered and require a long fuse. And yet he loves me. He knew what he was getting and signed up anyway. My best friend, best lover, and best playmate, Spence teaches me that there is a completely different way to live than what the statistics say I have a right to expect.

And I want to defy the odds for as long as we both shall live.

"Want to hit the backside again before we call it quits?" he asks.

"Sure," I say, "I'm just along for the ride."

CONNECTING

Essays from
True Words from Real Women

2010

BETWEEN US

Judy M. Miller

SHE CONNECTS YOU AND ME, two strangers, through the sacred bond of motherhood. We stand on either side of loss and grief. We stand on either side of her life's journey.

I respect you. I empathize with you. I will forever be thankful for the difficult decision you made. Without it, she would not be with me.

I love my child and so it is I love you as well, because you are part of her. You exist within every cell of her physical being. You exist deep within her memory stores. I'm sure of it. Some day she may want to know more, but for now she feels secure in her ingrained knowledge.

She has some of your characteristics and some of mine. She is Western and she is Eastern. She is poise, wit, and grace. She is ethical, committed to goals, and thoughtful. She is physically and emotionally strong. She is wise beyond her years, an old soul who knows who she is and is comfortable with herself.

You gave her life and overcame great obstacles to bring her into this world. You ushered her to safety, risking yours, so that she would end up within my loving arms.

I give her a home, unconditional love, and guidance. I laugh with her. Cry with her. And now, I hold her hand as she steps over the threshold to discover the mysteries of herself as she embarks on womanhood.

I wonder how you feel, as the years speed by, about the decision you had to make. I know, as a mother, you think of her continuously. I wish I could convey to you that she is content, balanced, joyous, and beautiful. She is deeply loved and cherished by her family.

Every time I look at the moon and stars, in the deep quiet of the night, I send prayers and thoughts your way, believing that you can feel my intentions and that they will find you healthy and happy. At peace.

She is our blessing. She is my heart and your soul. Born of you, adopted by me. Our daughter.

Making Connections

Linda Austin

My sister and I grew up listening to our Japanese mother tell us stories about her childhood spent growing up in a small town outside Tokyo. My mother was born in 1925 and, like many others of her era, endured the Depression during her formative years. She belongs in the ranks of parents who scrape the mayonnaise jars clean, who save every scrap of leftovers, and who demand that their children eat everything on their plates so as not to waste food.

Our mother's stories, though, did not dwell on the poverty she experienced. She told of childhood adventures and mishaps that, while from a different culture, we could relate to, as children worldwide play hide-and-seek, catch bugs, and occasionally get lost. On the other hand, the cultural difference made the stories even more fascinating to us, as we learned about the many festivals celebrated in Japan and listened with wide eyes to her mysterious "Old Fox" tales.

For the most part, my sister and I spent our time trying to fit into small-town American life despite our acorn-colored skin, the strange food we sometimes ate, and the silk kimonos hidden in footlockers. Somewhere in my teenage years, though, a seed was planted. I wanted to someday, somehow, record those stories of my mother's youth. I realized that they were indeed unusual and unique in our American world, which contained little other diversity at the time.

It wasn't until many years later, after I had married, moved several times, and had children, that I finally began writing down the stories of my mother's youth. My mother's friend, Frankie, started the project while my life was still busy and unsettled. One day Frankie handed me a computer disk containing whatever stories she had coaxed my mother to write in her broken English and that Frankie could manage to understand and type up. Thus began a beautiful journey.

The stories were gathered in spurts and bits and pieces over ten years. My mother was full of happy reminiscences and I collected her scraps of writing as well as the little drawings she would create to help me understand her stories. Mostly, though, since my mother never mastered the English language, I would quiz her, reminding her of the tales she told me as a child, asking her about the circumstances and her feelings about what happened. I would scribble down the answers and later type them up, often to think of even more questions to ask. Sometimes I had to beg her to tell me simple details of her life that she felt were insignificant and unimportant.

"Who cares about that?" she would say, annoyed.

"I do, and your grandchildren will," I would answer.

As I listened to my mother and pried my way into the hidden corners of her life, I began to understand more fully who she was. As a child, and especially as a teenager, I could not understand why she behaved in ways that seemed either irrational to me or, at least, unlike what I was used to from other adults in my life. I began to see how her early cultural learning affected her life in America, and how certain painful experiences had made their marks upon her. I remember sitting in the car with her, crying together, and I wish that I had known these things about her so much earlier, so that I would have been more patient and understanding with her.

A few years ago, my mother began losing her short-term memory. In the spring of 2005, I realized that I needed to work hard to finish the book before she was unable to help me anymore. I also saw reminders everywhere—on television, on radio, and in the newspapers—of the approaching sixtieth anniversary of the end of World War II, a significant event in her life. Those reminders nagged at me to hurry, because time was flying by and my mother was in her twilight years.

I worked with my mother almost daily for three months. By the time the book was finished, a month before her eightieth birthday, I felt a deep bond between us. Laughing and crying, questioning and learning, the little gulf that used to be between us had disappeared.

My mother was astonished to see how well our project together had turned out. She was thrilled to hold the beautiful book of her life in her timeworn hands. She is surprised and proud when people tell her how much they enjoyed and learned from her story. Most of all, she loves to turn the pages and relive precious moments over and over—treasures that will now never be lost.

CHILDBIRTH 1977

Karen Buley

I AM ABOUT TO WITNESS MY FIRST BIRTH. I am twenty; my patient and her husband are eighteen.

I am a third-year nursing student, no stranger to Saint James Community Hospital. At fourteen, I'd begun volunteering as a Candy Striper. My days then had been limited to the postpartum area, filling water pitchers and delivering flowers to new mothers. The doors to the labor and delivery unit had remained closed. I fantasized about being allowed in there some day.

That day has arrived.

I am in a tiny labor room, helping the young couple through the throes of labor. I know the Lamaze breathing method. We nursing students assisted in childbirth education classes. I devoured the books I borrowed from the RN instructor—my mother. But this is different; this is not reading, or teaching couples on the floor of the county health building.

I stand beside my patient's bed, stroking her legs and saying, "Breathe like this," demonstrating the "in-two-three-four, out-two-three-four" breaths we'd taught in the childbirth classes. Her husband sits on the opposite side of the bed in a straight-backed chair, a terrified look on his face.

When it is time to transfer my patient to the delivery room, her husband stays behind. Hospital rules in 1977. He hasn't attended childbirth classes, so he hasn't earned his ticket in.

As my patient pushes, I cradle her head. And when her new-born son emerges—blue, wet and slippery—I cry. For the beauty. For the miracle. And for her husband.

Confederation Farm

Kathi Kouguell

WE TOOK TWO WEEKS and drove many miles through Canada: New Brunswick, Nova Scotia, Prince Edward Island, Cape Breton, adventure and wonderful views around every corner. At the Bay of Fundy, we stood, waiting for the water to rise dramatically. We watched and waited until we finally understood that it would happen slowly over many hours. We laughed at ourselves for years.

One late afternoon in Nova Scotia, we decided to stop at a bed-and-breakfast for the night. That was how we first came across Confederation Farm—a simple farmhouse with a large barn to the right of it and land in back.

As we went upstairs to our room, we passed a small bookcase with some framed photographs on it. I peeked and saw a soldier in a Canadian uniform wearing a beret. I said to *M*, "Perhaps one day I will meet one of the soldiers who liberated my parents and me in Holland in 1945, and thank him face-to-face." We had an enjoyable stay there, leaving after two days without having had an opportunity to speak of it to the owner.

The following year we decided to return to Canada. One late afternoon, we found ourselves in the area of Confederation Farm. We decided to phone them and see if they had a room for the night. When Julia, the owner, answered, I gave her my last name, told her that we had been there the summer before, and that we were looking for a room. She immediately remembered us. She told me that they had no guests at the moment and we certainly could come.

When we arrived, she asked if we would like to join her and her husband for dinner after we had freshened up. We agreed. We passed the bookcase with the photos on the way to our room and I said to *M*, "Tonight, I am going to find out about that Canadian soldier."

Downstairs at the dinner table we met Julia's husband, Bob, and sat down to a simple but delicious dinner. I said to Bob that I had noticed the photograph upstairs and asked if that was a photo of him in the uniform.

He replied, "Yep." A man of few words.

I asked if he had been in the army during World War II. He replied, "Yep."

I asked if he had been in Europe. He replied, "Yep." By this time, *M* had turned on his little pocket recorder.

I asked Bob where he had been. He said, "Italy."

Something made me ask, "Anywhere else?"

He said, "Holland."

The hair on my arms rose. I asked him if he had been to Amsterdam in May of 1945. He replied, "Yep."

"Then you liberated the city," I said. I asked what he saw when they came in on their tanks and trucks.

"Well," he said slowly, "the sidewalks were full of people holding flowers and crying, and all the children were standing in the front."

I looked at him, tears streaming down my face. "I was one of those children. I have always wanted to meet one of you to thank you personally." We were all crying. Bob kept patting my arm. Julia left the table and we heard her banging pots and pans in the kitchen. Clearly, it had become too much for her.

After dinner, she asked if I would sit in the living room with her. She sat in her armchair and picked up her knitting. I was watching her when Bob came into the room. He said, "Thought you'd like to see this," and handed me a small piece of paper.

Julia said, "What's that, Bob?"

"This is my pass for R-and-R in a hotel in Amsterdam a few weeks after the liberation." She asked him where he had kept this and he said, "Strangest thing happened. This morning I was passing the bookcase upstairs, and my foot hit one of the books. This hotel pass fell out."

All the events of the past hours came rushing back to me: the sudden decision to stay at Confederation Farm; Julia remembering our name one year and many guests later; the vacancy; the photo; the dinner invitation; the conversation; the hotel pass falling out of a book, where it might have been for over forty years.

When we left the next morning, Bob insisted on showing us his barn where he had tables full of old tools and collectibles. As we said goodbye, we lingered some more, and then hugged and cried one last time.

THE PURPLE GOWN

Kira Janene Holt

I'VE NEVER WANTED FOR MUCH, been homeless, or starving. I've had parents and friends whose love I've felt, and the tribulations I've faced are of my own making. I've cried over men but rarely possessions. One of the times I did cry, it was over a purple satin gown.

Mother and I shopped one Saturday in Corpus at an upscale clothing store in the then vital downtown. The elevators stood etched in gold. A man turned the lever to take us to the women's floor. We must have been looking for something special for Mother, because my dresses came from Sears.

As Mom shopped, I lingered through pajamas, robes, and other apparel. That's when I spied it. The purple gown hung on a circular rack of sleepwear: a soft, lavender satin, with sheer voile of the same hue cut to cover the cloth. A matching voile robe completed the outfit. At its neck, two pompoms hung from cords that closed the robe and complimented short, puffed sleeves. The fabric draped luxuriously below the knees and I imagined the gown fit for a princess. I'd never been drawn to an article of clothing before but that gown called my heart.

I stared at the gown, eventually working up the courage to touch the softness of the fabric. I stroked it as I would a cat, or the mink my great aunt wore. I looked at the price tag: twenty dollars. An outrageous amount to pay for something a twelve-year-old girl would sleep in.

We weren't poor. Daddy drilled oil wells in the Gulf and around South Texas while Mother worked as an oil and gas secretary. Daddy made Mother put her paychecks into their savings account for retirement, but every so often she'd take one and spend it on what she wanted—the house, herself, my brother or me—and Daddy was wise enough to let her do it.

A saleswoman came and asked if I'd like to try on the gown. I'd been caught. At what, I'm not sure, but I shook my head in nervous embarrassment. She'd intruded into a private moment between me and the gown. When she left, I climbed between the gowns, into the middle of the circle of clothes, where nobody could see me. I continued petting the robe, gently moving its pompoms.

I didn't think to ask Mother to buy the robe. Buying it would have been silly, impractical, and a waste of money. I don't recall feeling unworthy of wearing something so lush—it was more that I didn't have the right to ask for what I didn't need.

I stayed with the gown until I heard Mother calling. I touched the fabric to my cheek and inhaled its new-clothes smell before stepping out of hiding.

Sadness for leaving the gown and shame for desperately wanting it enveloped me. I didn't know how to hide the feelings, new, powerful, and raw, and tears came. I wept silently and wiped the tears away before I joined Mother at the cashier's stand.

The silent tears wouldn't stop, hard as I tried to make them. The woman at the counter, the one who asked if I wanted to try on the gown, noticed, as did Mother. She asked what was wrong. It took me a moment to find my voice. I took her to the gown, pointed to it, and whispered, "It's so pretty." The tears spilled out.

My mother grabbed the ensemble off the rack. She looked at the price tag. She looked at me, handed me the hanger, and instructed me to try it on. She didn't follow.

I stood in the dressing room with the gown on, tying and untying the pompoms. While not transformed into a princess as imagined, I loved the coolness of the fabric against my skin. Mom asked from the other side of the curtain if it fit. I told her it did. She asked me to hand it to her, which I did, and by the time I finished putting on my real clothes, she'd purchased it. I felt conflicted—loving the gown but ashamed that I had cried. I thanked her for buying it for me, and she smiled.

I rarely wore the gown. I would bring it out when my bedroom door was shut, hold it against me, and dance around the room. It was too pretty to wear, and I was afraid I'd rip its sheerness. That gown could lift most any pre-adolescent funk. It and

46

the robe—long since outgrown—hung in my closet until I left for college.

I must have been forty when I asked Mother if she remembered the gown. She did. I told her how much I had loved it. She knew. I asked her why she bought it. She told me that I had never asked for anything. She could see how much it meant, and she wanted me to have it.

As I approach fifty, that gown still touches me. I can feel the satin against my skin, and flick imaginary pompoms, sending each flying to the end of its cord. I wish I still had the outfit, if only to see if it's still as beautiful as it is in my mind. Tears still come when I think about it. Now the tears are for the unending love of a mother who bought her daughter something beautiful—a princess outfit—when she didn't have to. In that kind gesture, without lecture, a mother silently honored the dignity of a daughter at the start of an awkward path to adulthood.

SAWDUST

Barbara Dee

PAPA TOOK ME OUT TO HIS WORKSHOP every evening after our early dinner. My grandmother never came with us. Maybe the arthritis in her knees was so bad that the five-minute walk was too much for her. Or maybe she didn't want to face her suspicion of what was going on out there.

Papa's shop was a gray cement-block building, which stood alone near the sidewalk's end, past the water tanks. Inside the shop were gray walls, brown wood, black tool handles. The smell of varnish hung in the hot sticky air. A black rubber mat on the gray cement floor was the only decor. A centered plywood table supported a lathe, its cold, metal machine voice steely silent. Sometimes the tabletop was covered with wood pieces and wide-jawed clamps, two-clawed hammers, jagged-tooth saws. Sometimes a freshly varnished captain's chair perched on the table as if it had jumped up there off the floor.

One hot, humid, July day, Papa was working on one of his famous teacarts. My big brother and I were together in Papa's shop, a rare event. My brother picked up a power tool off the worktable and examined it, turning it slowly in his hands. A stop sign flashed in my mind as if I had reached for the tool myself. I, of course, wasn't allowed to touch a power tool. "You got no business with that, little girl," I heard a scolding replay in my mind. I reached out and snatched the yardstick that was leaning against the workbench and clenched my hand as tight as my teeth.

"My new jigsaw," Papa explained to my brother. I held the yardstick, the worn wooden flat stick almost too big around for my grip. Tap, tap, tap. I tapped the edge on the cement floor next to the faded cane-back chair. Scrape, scrape, scrape. I dragged the stick through the shavings and sawdust and pushed up enough of it to make a tidy hill. I knew the shavings by heart. Each was a variation of blondish brown, each with a hundred edges. I knew the edges of the shavings, some sliced smooth, some rough torn. I knew the dust that covered the edges of the shavings, some fine and powder light, some coarse and as big as a splinter. Studying the sawdust was what I did, standing by the old cane-back chair for endless amounts of time—yesterday, the day before that, as long as I can remember. Only the creaking cane-back chair my grandfather sat in broke my keen concentration on the saw-dusty floor. My eyes, my mind, my soul, had been on that floor many, many times, so I knew it well.

In a slightly delayed reaction, I heard my brother's words, and was startled to realize they were directed at me. "Aunt Martha was lovin' her tea cart when we were there Sunday, wasn't she?" I looked up into his handsome face, noticing like always his beautiful, smooth skin—not your typical teenager skin, no blemishes, clean-shaven. His soft blue eyes connected with mine and held my look.

I nodded the expected response and said, "Uh-huh." He unlocked our eyes and went back to his friendly conversation with the diseased man he was immune to.

My eyes drifted and stopped on Papa's straw hat hanging on the wall. I put one bended knee on the chair's seat and pressed it down hard to lift myself to reach the edge of the hat. With the hat in my hand, I walked away from the chair and sat down on the floor. I scraped the edge of my small, cupped hand along the cold, rough floor. I closed it around one tiny mound and then the next, and filled the bottom of the upside down hat with sawdust, wood chips, and dusty shavings off the floor.

"Papa," I interrupted my brother. I held the hat out to Papa. "Put on your hat, Papa," I said. With no hesitation, he took the hat from my hands and turned it over while putting it on top of his big, sweaty head. The insides dumped out. Fine dust, coarse shavings, and dirty scrapings rained down over his sweaty brow and nose. A cloud of sawdust covered his entire face, and the tiny chips stuck there, or fell to his shoulders. He squinted and blinked his eyes, his eyelashes now covered in coarse, yellow dust.

My brother screamed at me, "I've never seen anyone do anything so *mean!*" His face was red and his voice shook with anger.

I looked at the shavings and dust covering Papa's tightly closed eyes. He sputtered to blow the sticky shavings off his lips and mouth. He reached up with one large, mottled-skin hand and removed the hat from his head. More dust rained from his mouse-grey hair onto his shoulders, which had started to slump forward.

Shame burned my eyes and made them water. I hated what had just happened, but I hated Papa more. I stared at Papa. He looked pathetic. Instead of feeling sorry, I started feeling a rush. I felt triumphant and, finally, in control.

Papa never said a word.

PLAYING WITH DOLLS

Johnett Scogin

THE LAST YEAR I BELIEVED IN SANTA CLAUS, I asked for, and got, my favorite baby doll ever—Baby Tender Love. Baby Tender Love was the flight simulator for mommies in training. She came with little pink and yellow clothes and adorable pink booties. Her hair was the blond color that I later came to associate with former high school cheerleaders. She had blue eyes, a cute button nose, and a little pink bow of a mouth with a hole in it just big enough to accept the "drink and wet" bottle (patent pending). But my favorite thing about Baby Tender Love was that her skin was not made of hard vinyl or stuffed cotton but some sort of foam polymer that was soft and yielding. That, and her skin was infused with the scent of baby powder, so it made you want to hold her close, stroking her chubby little arms, inhaling the perfume of motherhood.

As I grew a bit older, Baby Tender Love gave way to Barbie fashion dolls, though I usually preferred Skipper or Midge to the buxom star of the show. Along with my sister and friends, I whiled away entire rainy afternoons making up dramas about parties and dates and Barbie's inevitable marriage to Ken. I could imagine the white dress, the flowers, and Ken with his perfect smile, smart blue-velvet tuxedo, and molded-in-place Rick Perry hairstyle.

One year, my sister asked for a board game for her birthday called "The Bride Game." The goal was to move around the board, collecting cards for all the necessary pieces of the wedding. First stop was the bridal gown (even before the groom). You never knew which dress would be the one you drew, but all of us wanted the gorgeous "formal evening" wedding with the most ornate gown, flowing veil, beautiful bouquet of flowers, bridesmaids' dresses, and the handsomest groom.

I bet I played that game a hundred times that year. I knew every bridal gown and her mate. I listened to my sister and friends go into great detail describing their ideal wedding day, and the criteria they currently had for Mr. Right. I could see each girl in turn parading down the aisle arm-in-arm with her father, Mendelssohn blaring on the pipe organ. In every wedding, I was a bridesmaid or the maid of honor, but even in my imagination, I was never the girl getting married.

Somehow, I knew from a very young age that I wasn't cut out for this marriage-and-kids thing. The whole idea of it just seemed farcical when applied to me. My sisters and girlfriends never questioned their roles as wife and mother, even if they also wanted to become doctors or lawyers, or high-powered businesswomen. For them the mold seemed to fit. But somewhere on a cellular level, I just knew: I would never marry or become a mother.

At first, that lack of desire for motherhood was neutral, but by adolescence, the idea took on a decidedly more negative tone. Of *course* I wasn't getting married. Who in their right mind would want me? In elementary school, I was the smart fat kid. By middle school I was the pimply fat girl, the one who might know all the answers in class but who was destined never to be more than a sidekick in her friends' romantic adventures.

By high school, my fate was sealed. I was a brain. My best friends were the head majorette and a semi-closeted gay boy every bit as shy as I was. It made for an odd triangle, but it sort of worked for me. I got to watch my girlfriend's romantic milestones and missteps and live vicariously through her dates, her loves, and her breakups. And my gay friend and I were comfortable being together. We were soul mates, and helped each other out by going to proms and banquets together. He was my beard—or I was his. We never quite figured that out, even after he came out of the closet to me after he spent two years in the Army. (Don't ask, don't tell.)

So, the one man I had ever truly loved was not going to be my husband either, though one Saturday he did propose to me, saying we could get away from both of our families and make a life of our own. We knew it wouldn't have worked, but now that he's been gone for almost eight years, dead from AIDS, it is a particularly bittersweet memory.

My lack of romantic involvement was rarely something I dwelled on. It wasn't going to happen for me. Why should it? And since most of my married friends (including both of my sisters) had been through at least one divorce, remaining single seemed to have been a smart decision, if unintentionally so.

But then, the impossible happened. I fell in love with someone who was in love with me. It didn't matter that my love was another woman. The feeling was still the same, and still as miraculous. That we have been living together as a couple, married in our eyes if not those of the State, for almost five years is something I celebrate daily and thank all the powers of the Universe for allowing me to experience.

Maybe, all those years ago, if I could have envisioned Skipper and Midge all grown up and married to each other, living in Massachusetts with a Subaru station wagon and three adopted kids, it might have occurred to me sooner that I could have a lasting love that didn't look like other partnerships I had seen. But then again, maybe not. And maybe my own marriage is all the more special for it.

SWEEPSTAKES

Susan C. Williams

BACK IN THE 1980s, my dad was caught up in the annual television-generated excitement of entering publishing company sweepstakes. Every year, he was absolutely convinced he was going to win. He was never discouraged when someone else was surprised at their front door with the giant check and flowers and balloons, as shown on TV commercials. Once, he got a computer-generated letter saying, "A limo could be pulling up to your front door on January 28." He told my mom they had to be sure and stay home that day. "But it has my name on it!" he'd say when we teased him for falling for these ploys. My young daughter, caught up in her granddad's enthusiasm, began retrieving the sweepstakes mailings from our trash can at home, carefully affixing the stickers and proudly mailing her entries by the deadline. The selection of magazines available in both our houses grew.

Daddy, who ran his own business, was always open to a new way of building his bank account. Like the year he bought 2,000 baseball caps from a friendly entrepreneur on a street corner in Louisville, Kentucky, several hours and drinks after the Kentucky

Derby. Under the embroidered "1982 Kentucky Derby" on the hat was a pocket with a tiny transistor radio, so you could listen to the broadcast of the horse race while "watching" it from the infamous infield. Mom and I voiced astonishment and exasperation when the caps were delivered. But he had a plan: take the hats to Knoxville, Tennessee, and set up a street stand near the 1982 World's Fair. My argument that no one wanted to spend his souvenir money on a Kentucky Derby hat at the World's Fair was brushed aside. He was outraged when local street vendor laws killed the plan. In 1993, when he and Mom sold the house they'd lived in for 42 years and moved to a retirement community, we found 1,953 of the caps still in boxes in the garage.

After sending in various entry forms each year, Daddy then became obsessed with his projected sweepstakes winnings. He spent hours at the kitchen table writing notes on a yellow legal pad about ways to spend his five million dollars. When the grand prizes reached figures like twenty million dollars, he was nearly beside himself. He bought more legal pads. Sound sleep eluded him as he tossed and turned, trying to think of enough ways to spend all the money. "I always have some left over," he'd report with frustration the next day, and then he'd pull out his legal pad to adjust figures.

A couple of years before Daddy died, I asked to see his yellow legal pad for the current sweepstakes season. I'm glad I did; it changed the way I saw him. That day a man with a generous spirit and nature was revealed to me, one who—if he'd had the financial resources—would have been a philanthropist.

That day, I saw columns of figures and interest calculations, timelines and project descriptions, all in his flowing Palmer Method cursive writing. So sure was he of winning that he'd consulted his attorney to find out how to establish a charitable foundation.

My sister and I were to be the foundation's officers and draw a salary. ("So you won't be a bag lady," he said to me.) There was something for Mom, of course, and for my daughter's college education, and gifts for his sisters and their kids, and a few other things I no longer remember. But the majority of funds and earnings would give rural kids a leg up when it came to college.

My dad's formal education ended with the eighth grade, not uncommon in rural Tennessee in the 1920s. He was expected to help provide for their large family. Daddy told me once that when the family of ten moved after losing their farm, he and his brother constructed a shelter of heavy cardboard and slept on the streets of downtown Louisville, Kentucky, so they'd hear the newspaper bundles being dropped on the sidewalks at four a.m. and could hit the streets first and make the most sales. For the rest of his life, Daddy was up early and trying to beat the competition by getting there first.

Daddy became a successful businessman, but he never got over the fact that he'd left school so young. I think it embarrassed him, but he tried to hide that by cracking jokes about graduating from The School of Hard Knocks and saying that he had married my mom because "she had a college education and a fur coat." The plan to use his sweepstakes prize to help other rural children go to college and avoid his experience was touching. And though he never won twenty million dollars, he did eventually make a generous gift to the scholarship fund of a nearby university.

A few months after Daddy died, my mom opened an envelope addressed to him. Inside was a letter that said, "You've won," along with a check for two hundred dollars.

TRUSTING MY CHILDREN, TRUSTING MYSELF

Margaret Stephenson

SNUGGLING WITH MY NINE-YEAR-OLD DAUGHTER, Kaley, early in the morning during winter break from school, I am surprised to hear her announce, "I want to homeschool!" I have savored these three weeks of rare, uninterrupted time together building fires, playing games, taking warm baths, and talking late into the night with my husband and our three young children.

"You love school. Do you really want to homeschool?" I ask Kaley.

"I don't love school. *You* love my school. It's so crowded I can't even think, I already know everything they're teaching, and it's boring. I don't have any time to do what I want to do, like read Harry Potter and learn Greek," she blurts out like she's prepared this speech.

"Well, what about Samantha and Victoria and art and violin?" I ask.

"I'll make new friends and have play dates. I could do all kinds of art on my own and I could take music lessons," she says.

"But you love Mrs. Woods," I say without much conviction as my daughter's words begin to seep through my defenses. I am flooded with recent memories of her sitting at home reading on the couch after school, not wanting to talk or do anything but relax into her book for hours. I see the stiffening of her body and the hardening of her eyes as she slowly steps out of the van and walks to her classroom. And what about the daily stomachaches that I've come to accept as part of her? I try to believe it when her teacher says these things are normal.

"I like Mrs. Woods, but I like you more," she says.

"Why don't we do some research and if we all think it's a good idea, maybe we can homeschool, but we need to think about it some more," I say. I'm excited by her idea and, at the same time, I wonder if by opening this door I am harming her.

I have to make a decision. My oldest wants to leave school and I suspect my two younger ones will follow her lead. Do I assume that my daughter knows her own mind and is making a wise decision? Do I listen to her teacher, who thinks my daughter is doing well in school, even though she admits she looks "frail" in the classroom? Do I listen to the public school administrator, the one that whispers the word "homeschool" with pinched lips? What about my school nurse friend who says kids who have been homeschooled are behind, academically and socially? Do I listen to my husband who supports the idea, my friends who say if anyone can do it I can, and my several homeschooling friends who ask why I waited so long? Do I listen to my own thoughts that have hastily fast-forwarded to the fun and freedom we could have as homeschoolers?

I collect opinions. I ask the cashier at Starbucks who says she homeschooled, my neighbor, my best friend, the old high school friend I've reconnected with on Facebook. Then I stir in every book on homeschooling I can find and add a pinch of information from education and curriculum e-mail lists. It's like I'm playing a game of Twister, left hand on green, right foot on blue, hoping I won't tumble. I spend countless hours on the Internet in the wee hours of the morning trying to figure this out, until the information starts repeating itself and I can breathe. I let it marinate for a few months, until I become comfortable with what my daughter knew was right for her and homeschooling becomes a reality.

When my daughter cried as a baby, I carried her, fed her, or slept by her side. I held her hands and talked with her as she learned to walk and speak. She intuitively learned to trust herself and know that her needs were important as I listened and responded. Why do I question whether she knows what she needs at age nine?

Almost three years have passed since my daughter declared she wanted to homeschool and we embarked on this winding journey with all three kids through homeschooling groups, theater companies, children's choirs, horse shows, dance classes, and writing groups. We've explored and discarded countless curricula, and I've found the courage to mostly let them follow their interests, against a wall of constant internal questioning about whether I'm doing the right thing.

My anxiety comes out in bursts of control; I have them try yet another math curriculum, take a writing class they don't really want to take, or have them stick with violin because they made a commitment.

I want my kids to know how to think and make good decisions, but mostly, I want them to trust themselves. I will perform an experiment; I'm going to see what happens if I trust my children without doubting myself. I'm going to grant myself permission to let go of the background noise that sabotages my efforts to respect my children's needs and let them think and make their own decisions. I want them to see me trusting myself. I'll start my experiment now, document my progress, and know that I can always bring back the angst if I decide life works better that way.

REMEMBERING

Essays from
True Words from Real Women

2011

REMEMBERING AUGUST, 1959, NORTHERN WISCONSIN

Susan Flemr

DEAR BOB,

On the dock, after we counted falling stars for an hour or more in remarkable silence broken only occasionally by a wailing loon, you asked, "What would you say if I kissed you?"

You didn't wait for my answer. You reached for my shoulders, turned me toward you, and pressed your lips gently into mine, for a brief time.

My response came as my cheek nestled into your shoulder. "I would say thank you," I responded in a shaky whisper, as the steam from my breath and tears collided with the cold August night air.

Those warm tears sent the fragrance of your plaid wool jacket into my nostrils. I can still smell that warm, wet wool now, some fifty years later.

I understood that the kiss was your gift to me. We stood clinging tightly to each other, on wobbly legs. Both trembling. Me, because my teenage fantasy had come true. You, because you had never kissed a girl and were learning that you probably wouldn't be kissing many more.

Your tears soaked through my long hair, wetting my ear as you whispered, "I do love you, Susan." I heard your struggle to convey the great unspoken meaning in those words.

Neither of us completely understood, but we did. You were gay. Only we didn't say *gay* in the 50s.

I refuse to use the word *queer*. I think that was the descriptive word used then. There were other things said behind your back at school because you avoided team sports, enjoyed classical music, and were a top scholar. All those things made you attractive to me. The boys secretly laughed about your effeminate mannerisms. I saw you as gentle and caring.

This was the final night of our last summer vacation before you went off to college and I returned for two more years of high school. The two weeks we spent each of the past five years would now be memories I would relive every time I heard the song "Twilight Time," ate freshly-picked blueberries, swam in a cold northern lake, or thought of that longed-for kiss.

Each year you came running to find me the minute your family car was unpacked, and for two weeks each summer we were inseparable. We hiked miles on dirt roads, smelling the pine and finding scrubby patches of wild blueberries. We would fill our metal pans full of berries and proudly bring them home to our families for breakfast. We spent hours swimming, catching frogs, building sand castles, playing board games on rainy days, and talking about our dreams.

You admonished me never to worry about my height, weight, or appearance, and encouraged me to just be true to myself. That was a novel thought for me at the time—a message you repeated over and over. I understood later that you desperately needed to hear it, too.

After graduating at the top of your high school class, you went off to college, graduate school, then on to teaching and writing. You published well-documented and well-received books. You lived in Greenwich Village, Manhattan, New York.

You died at forty-three and your memorial service was held at St. John's-in-the-Village Episcopal Church. This church now has an active ministry to gay and lesbian youth struggling with their place in this world. Yes, dear Bob, young men and women still struggle as you did on that dock so many years ago.

May our world answer their tears with more than bullying words and the lonely wail of the loon.

With love,
Susan

CODE BLUE

Julia Atwood

I WAS ONCE ASKED, "If your life had a shape or pattern what would it look like?" Without skipping a beat, I replied, "The EKG of a heart attack."

It is a warm September day in 1968. I am twelve years old, out of sorts with my body, skinny and awkward. They call me "spider legs" at school. I am flat chested and my teeth are crooked with white calcium deposits that make the rest look yellow. I don't smile. My father does not believe in braces and what my father says is law.

My mother has cut my hair in a pixie because she thinks it is stylish and cute. I hate my hair, my body, my face, and my twelve-year-old life. I am not beautiful. I am not even cute. Nothing about me looks like a woman. I look and dress like a boy. I argue with my mother more now because with this new cut I look even more like a boy. I want to wear frilly dresses, ribbons in my long hair, socks with lace around the ankles, strappy black shoes, and carry a handbag. I want to grow up.

My father, a tall handsome man with piercing blue eyes and chiseled jaw, has a flattop haircut, and looks just like Clint Eastwood. For all his rugged charm and physical prowess, he is mean-tempered and cruel. He is both dangerous and alluring.

My mother is a willow of a woman with warm brown eyes, thick dark hair, ruby red lips and a radiant smile. She looks like Snow White. She wears cinch-waisted cotton dresses with cashmere cardigans and matching kitten pumps. She pulls her hair back with a thick plastic hair band, which highlights her angular face. She wears pearl post earrings and a single strand of pearls around her neck. My mother is an elegant housewife. She cooks the best fried chicken in all Mono County.

I think my parents are movie-star beautiful. I am hoping I will someday turn out as attractive as they are.

As I walk home from school, I am thinking that when I get home I will ask my mother if I can try on her wedding dress. Every year I get to take it out of her cedar chest and try it on to see if it fits. I stand on a chair and look in the mirror. I imagine how I will look when I fit into all the hollow spaces.

The second I open the door I am hit with a hot silence that is deafening. I can hear the ticking of the clock. I can hear a faucet drip in the bathroom and the whirling ceiling fan. I can hear ringing in my ears. There is a frightening and profound emptiness permeating the house, a feeling of violation. I walk into the kitchen. The dishes are washed and stacked in the drainer. The dishtowels folded. Counters are wiped, floors swept, rugs in place.

In the living room the carpet has been freshly vacuumed with the Electrolux vacuum my mother purchased from a door-to-door salesman, and for which she received a split lip and a broken nose, which blackened both her eyes. There are straight lines etched side by side exactly eighteen inches wide and three feet long made by the new agitating feature of the Deluxe model she had purchased.

I was there to hear the whole sales pitch so I know the exact specifications. I'd sat mystified as the salesman gave me a cup of dark brown dirt to throw onto the carpet. I looked at my mother as if to say, "Can I really do this?" With her arms folded in speculation and defiance, she nodded okay. I dumped the dirt on the carpet.

"Grind it in there, really make it hard for me," he'd said. I looked back to my mother. She was growing concerned. If this didn't work, she would have to clean it up; she would have to explain to my father. I held my breath. I thought I saw her sweating, heard her heart beating. I ran my shoe hard back and forth across the dirt-filled carpet. In a not quite panicky, but measured tone, she declared, "That's enough!"

With the showmanship and hand gestures of a magician on the Ed Sullivan Show, he'd activated the magic agitating wand. "The dirt easily and completely disappears," he'd said in his showiest, authoritative voice. I could feel his power. It was almost holy.

I was sold. I was a believer. I begged, "Can we buy it, Mommy? Please!" Between him and me, she was defenseless. She got out her checkbook, hesitated, and then, with quiet determination, she wrote a check. She did not consult my father on such a large purchase. Even I knew this was dangerous business.

I walk through the living room and down the hall. In the bathrooms, the porcelain sinks are spotless, the stainless steel faucets sparkle, and the bathtubs are ring-less from our previous night's baths. It smells of Pine Sol and Windex. Navy blue towels hang neatly side by side. Everything is in perfect order yet something is missing.

I walk into my parents' bedroom. The closet is open and half empty. I spin to look at the dresser. Her perfumes and Jean Naté powder are gone. I look under the bed. Both pieces of the Samsonite luggage are gone. On my father's pillow is a note in precise hand-written script.

Doug, I cannot take it anymore. You can keep everything. Do not look for me. I am done. — Joan

I stand there in my budding womanhood, holding in my hands the only goodbye I would see from her. My heart skips a beat. Stops. Then breaks.

SUMMER FLIGHT

Amber Lea Starfire

FIFTEEN MINUTES INTO A TWENTY-MINUTE FLIGHT from Denver to Colorado Springs, darkness closed in on us. When we'd lifted off the tarmac, the clear sky held only a few scattered clouds. Now, thunderclouds wrapped around us and the sky went black. We could barely see the tips of our wings. Rain and hail pounded the windshield. Our one-engine plane dipped and rose and tipped, my stomach flip-flopping with it. Veins stood out like blue cords on my mother's hands as she fought to control the plane, which rocked from side to side like a toy in the hands of a great, malevolent monster.

Jagged knives of lightning pierced the darkness, accompanied by explosions of thunder. I screamed, covered my ears, certain we would be torn to pieces and scattered over the landscape below. In the seat behind me, my ten-year-old brother Michael was either yelling or laughing maniacally. I couldn't tell for the din of the storm.

My mother decided to try to outrun the tempest. Aiming the nose of the plane toward a thin grey line on the horizon, she flew the Piper Cherokee 180 as fast as it would go—125 miles an hour. But the storm clamped its jaws around us.

Four days before, on June 16, 1967, we had posed for local reporters before taking off in our rented one-engine Piper for a two-month tour of the United States. We were a photogenic threesome: my mother trim in her brown leather flight jacket and short wavy hair; me, prepubescent and awkward, standing close to my mother, emulating her confidence; Michael, in jeans and short-sleeved, button-down shirt, scowling against the sun.

In those days, a woman flying solo across the U.S. with two children was daring. Before we left, my mother had shrewdly promoted us, gaining sponsorships from aviation companies, hotels, and resorts, which in turn would benefit from the publicity we brought to them. We'd spent that morning with journalists and the president of an aviation map company, delaying our takeoff until midafternoon. Before now, my mother had not realized that flying so late in the day could be perilous.

"Look for a place to land," my mother yelled over the roar of the wind and rain. "A field, a road, anything!" Her arms strained and trembled as she continued to battle the storm. Glad to have something to do, Michael and I squinted through the darkness. Sometimes, we could make out the faint outlines of fences, the green and yellow of fields thick with corn. We'd been flying for over two hours and had no idea where we were.

"Dear God, please don't let my children die!" I heard Mom say. "I'll do anything, just let us get through this."

I stared at her open-mouthed. My mother was an atheist. Hearing her pray terrified me more than anything that had happened so far. Always in control, she belied fear even to herself, fiercely attacking anything that tried to hold her back from what she wanted. And she always won. I had never heard her plead or bargain—let alone with a god whom she did not believe existed—in any of the risky situations we'd been in during our travels around the world two years before. I'd never doubted my mother's ability to keep us safe. Now, hearing her pray undermined everything I had thought to be sure. If my mother didn't know how to get out of this situation, then no one did, and we might really die.

"Look!" Michael yelled, pointing. He'd spotted a small airstrip with a red-roofed hanger and a few planes.

On our first two approaches, the wind blew us right off the runway. On the third try, we approached as if to land on the gravel to the left of it. We touched down. The plane rocked and bounced, threatening to veer off into the ruts of the ploughed field next to the strip, but we were on the ground! We taxied to a tie-down spot, pushed open the door, and struggled to hook the chains to the wings with our small hands. Rain drenched us and the wind pulled at our clothes and hair.

Grabbing our shared overnight case, we ran to the small airport office. It was closed, so we walked to the country road that fronted the airport—empty as far as we could see—and waited. After a short time, a battered red and white truck came in our direction. We stuck out our thumbs.

The truck stopped and a man with a deeply tanned and lined face rolled down the window. "Climb in," he said. The three of us crammed into the front seat, water draining onto the floorboards and into the upholstery.

"I saw you come down," he said. "Thought you might be in some trouble and came to take a look."

I thought that was just about the nicest thing I'd ever heard. The man told us we were still in Colorado, in Las Animas, about 125 miles southeast of Colorado Springs, and drove us to the nearest motel.

Getting ready for bed, Michael teased me about being afraid. Holding his head in his hands and rolling his eyes up so that all we could see were the whites, he pretended to scream. "Aaah! Aaah!" he wailed. "We're going to die! We're going to die!"

I threw a pillow at him. "You were scared, too, you little liar!" But I started to laugh, because he was right, and because it all seemed so funny now.

Mom laughed, too. I tried to tease her about praying. "I did not!" she said. Her still trembling hands betrayed her, but the denial comforted me: it felt like the mother I believed in had returned, and that mother would never admit that she'd been scared enough to pray.

THE WATCHER

Teri Heard Ralbovsky

As I PACE SHIN-DEEP NEAR THE WATER'S EDGE, cooling off in the water for a few minutes, I watch my seven-year-old son splash and swim with his friends a few yards away. Standing sentinel like this, a school of sunfish swimming around my legs, reminds me of a day in late summer, very much like this one—white clouds brushed across a robin's egg blue sky with a light breeze providing a respite from the intensity of the sun—when Mom parked underneath the maple tree, our usual spot, not far from the water's edge.

Before our station wagon settled into park, Mary and I had the doors open, jumping out, bare legs tearing away from the hot vinyl bench seat with the ripping sound and subsequent sting of a Band-Aid torn away from tender skin. Barefoot, dressed in matching green-and-mustard, floral-patterned, baby-doll bikinis with little ruffles on the bloomers, we raced each other across the dry, prickly late-summer grass to the water's edge, while Mommy finished unloading the car.

The afternoon stretched out lazily before us, an indulgent blend of flavors and textures: the salty-sweet taste of my greasy fingers as I licked the last of Mommy's cornflake-coated picnic chicken from them; the slippery tickle of the sunfish that swam around my legs as I waded near the shore; the cool silkiness of the water against my skin; and the warm caress of the sun on my face and shoulders, like a reassuring hand, as I popped up out of the water.

Like baby seals, Mary and I spent hours chasing each other in the water doing flips and underwater somersaults. When we were tired, we'd drag our bodies, beaded with water, up onto the warm, hard surface of the dock to sun ourselves.

I don't remember what Mom did. As I do today, she probably paced the shore. Maybe she dipped my infant brother, Larry, gently in and out of the water or supported his little body to float gently on its surface for his first swimming lessons. Maybe she read while he napped—one eye on the page, the other on us—much as I have today, never really free of duty as watcher.

However, I do remember the sound of her voice calling us: "Girls," high pitched and singsong, breaking the silence of late afternoon when the din of other children splashing and playing and the roar of motorboats subsided. She stretched out the one syllable word to two so it sounded more like *gir-rels.*

Eyes closed, waterlogged, we dozed in the late afternoon sun on the warm dock. Rocked gently in rhythm with the soft breeze, tiny waves splish-splashed against the side. Her call startled us out of our half sleep. Summoned, we slipped back into the cool late-afternoon water and swam to shore.

Mom greeted us with soft bath towels. "You two are little brown berries," she cooed as she rubbed dry our sun-bleached hair and bronzed skin. Sunscreen was not a part of our summer wardrobe in those days.

She left us seated on the picnic blanket, wrapped snugly in our towels and Larry asleep between us. Calling over her shoulder, "Teri, you're in charge," she walked toward the water for a quick dip. After a day of watching and waiting, it was her turn to swim away, briefly freed of her role of watcher, the mantle temporarily passed on to me.

The water had darkened to a deep blue—almost black—flecked with golden shards of sunlight that glinted back at me like the eye of a snake. As I watched Mommy's slender legs being swallowed inch by inch as she waded away from shore, I hugged my knees to my chest. When she reached the spot where the skirt of her bathing suit floated around her waist like a tutu, she drew her slender arms up into a triangle over her head and dove underneath the surface, swallowed whole by the dark water.

My tummy got that sick feeling deep down.

A shallow breath in and out until her head and arms broke the surface of the water. Using long, straight, slow strokes, she swam toward the rope in the middle of the lake where boats had sped back and forth trailing water skiers earlier that day.

We weren't allowed to swim out that far; it wasn't safe, Mommy told us. She didn't say why, but I guessed it was because the giant clam lived out there. That's why there was a rope marking the spot. No swimming, only boats.

Based on the size of the area that was roped off, the clam must have been huge, even bigger than the one we'd seen at the Natural History Museum in Cleveland a few weeks ago, the one that was so large that both Mary and me could curl up inside.

Mommy was halfway to the rope. I glanced sideways at Mary. Her head was resting on her knees, more tummy sickness like when I swing too high on the swing. Mommy kept swimming. She was getting smaller and smaller and I had to scrunch my eyes to see her head just above the water's surface.

Maybe she'd turn back now.

Larry started fussing. I put my hand on his belly and gently rolled him from side to side like a little dough ball. *Turn back now, Mommy*, I said inside my head. But she was still swimming away. Larry fussed louder. I felt for the pacifier, but couldn't look away from the water. I found it and found his mouth.

When Mommy reached the rope, stopped, turned and then dove beneath the surface, I sucked in my breath and started counting—*one two three four five*—until her head and arms broke the surface of the water. Exhaling belly flutters, I watched her swim long, straight, slow strokes back to us.

THE POWER OF PEBBLES

Cathy Marie Scibelli

IN THE SUMMER OF MY NINTH YEAR, I decided I had to have a Pebbles Flintstone doll. I have no recollection why this happened. Maybe a clever advertising campaign got inside my head and brainwashed me. Or perhaps one of my friends received the doll as a birthday present. Whatever the reason, I wanted that doll very badly, and the quest to get my parents to buy her became almost an obsession.

I tried to bring up the Pebbles Flintstone doll at every opportunity and I was not subtle. I cut a picture of it out of a magazine ad and hung it on my bedroom wall. I would say goodnight to the picture each evening when my mother came to tuck me in, and I remember one night patting the sheet next to me and saying, "Wouldn't it be nice if I had the Pebbles doll there to cuddle?" I would line up my other dolls and tell them, when a parent was in hearing distance, how Pebbles would be joining our family one day soon. I set a place for her at my little dolly tea table.

Whenever one of my parents would walk into the living room while I was watching the Flintstones cartoon, I would say something like, "Isn't Pebbles cute? I just love her." One day while my mother was ironing, I walked back and forth, then in and out of the room, until she asked, "What are you doing?"

"I'm imagining how much fun it would be to push my Pebbles doll in my doll carriage," I told her.

Looking back, I admire my persistence in light of the huge obstacle I faced. My mother was a thrifty New Englander who couldn't rationalize the idea of spoiling a child with something she considered a "big present" for no special occasion. Ice cream pops, a little Golden book, or a fifteen-cent Disneykin toy were "no occasion" treats.

"A doll is a birthday or Christmas present," she explained to me very clearly whenever I brought up the subject. "You don't need a doll now. If you still want it by Christmas, we'll see." My father offered no opinion whenever he heard my mother say this, so I assumed he agreed. Nevertheless, with the relentless optimism of childhood, I continued my campaign for several weeks.

Then one night my father pulled into the driveway after work and got out of the car holding a big bag in his hands. My mother was in the yard stoking the charcoal on our barbecue. "What's that?" she asked, gesturing to the bag as my father went over to kiss her.

"Just something," he answered, and grinned at me where I sat petting my cat under our apple tree.

Somehow, instinctively I knew what the "something" was and I jumped up and ran over to my father. "Let me see!" I yanked on his arm and he handed me the bag. As soon as I peeked inside, I saw the box with the lettering "Pebbles." I pulled it out yelling, "Yay!" and reached up to hug my father.

My mother gave him one of those looks and asked, "What did you do that for?" He just grinned and shrugged.

Nearly fifty years later, I can't remember much about any other doll I had. I remember very few of their names. I know I had Thumbelina because I remember the wind-up mechanism on her back never worked right and she didn't roll over the way she was supposed to. I had a doll named Blabby that made a weird noise that sounded like "Wack-oo" when you squeezed her stomach. I'm pretty sure I had a Chatty Cathy doll, too, because I remember people teasing me about the doll when it came out. I don't know if I received those dolls for Christmas or my birthday and I don't remember playing with them.

But I remember how special I felt when my father bought me that Pebbles doll for no apparent reason other than he knew it was something I really wanted. I carried it around, slept with it, and played with it for several years, and still regret that I gave it away when I was in high school and felt I was too old to have dolls decorating my room. Whenever I think of that moment when he presented me with that doll, I can still see his grin and his eyes meeting mine in that conspiratorial way.

My father died forty years ago, but the loving bond he created in that one act in that one moment will never die.

THE COLORS OF CHRISTMAS

P. Jan Hall

WHEN I WAS A LITTLE GIRL, Christmas was always bright and gold. My heart beat faster as each day of December passed—snail-slow in the beginning, then much too quickly. As the Special Day approached, Christmas Eve was the most difficult day. *Had I been good? Had I said my prayers? Helped Grandpa around the house enough? Suppose I forgot something—would Santa still come?* My little mind spun like a top. *What if . . . ?*

My teen years brought changes in how I felt about Christmas, subtle in the beginning, then like waves of midnight blue the day I discovered a closet full of goodies and realized everything there was what I asked Santa for. I was crushed, my heart broken. It seems I cried for days. On Christmas morning I broke Grandpa's heart; I refused to open a single present or speak to him because I'd learned that Santa was a lie. I knew I'd hurt Grandpa because he took a long walk without me—something he'd never done before. And the presents under the tree? Sometime later I relented and took them to my room where I opened them sadly. I eventually told Grandpa, "Thanks," and gave him a hug, but I could tell his feelings were still a little bruised.

Adulthood was almost-bright, tempered with reds and greens. My foster-kids brought Christmas out of the shadows as I saw my child-self in them. *Was I good? Did I help out enough? You heard me say my prayers every night, didn't you? Will Santa be able to find me here? I hope Mama's not lonely . . ."*

I did my best to lift them up and wipe away their tears. Sometimes it worked; other times it didn't. Either way, Christmas morning made everything right. As I watched their joy and wonder and appreciation for even the smallest gift, I learned anew the simple happiness of the season.

Now, in my sixty-second year, this special season brings a kaleidoscope of colors that have changed again. The bright gold of childhood is still there but muted; the midnight-blue waves of my teen years lap at a distant shore. The reds and greens of adulthood and foster-kids are the most noticeable, given an infusion of life because of an orange and white kitty, an almost-daughter, and a golden-haired seven-year-old with an ancient soul.

One new color has joined the spectrum, though: a sometimes-sad blue-ness that surrounds an empty chair in my heart. I don't yet know if I like this new color, but I am learning to accept it one day at a time, hoping against hope that the blue-ness will gradually soften into a gentle light-ness of spirit as I journey toward a new one-ness.

EARLY MORNING SONATA
AT BEEMER'S POND

Susanna Schuerman

THE CURTAIN RISES TO UNVEIL A BARREN TREE quivering in the wind, a rich hint of a cold, crisp day. I throw the blankets over my head and try to ignore the excited chatter of my photographer-husband, "Get up. We must get there before the birds fly out."

Hmmm. Bill didn't get the memo that this is a vacation day, meant for sleeping in, drinking hot tea in my jammies, or reading a mystery while wrapped in Grandma's handmade quilt—in other words, hibernating. There's no use arguing. We're heading out, and soon.

We are traveling to Beemer's Pond to photograph trumpeter swans. The hour-and-a-half drive is sprinkled with talk of Iowa's autumn landscape. Amber waves of grain have turned to brown rows of stubble this November day. We have not yet received a blanket of snow to cover the monochrome palette. We spot a red-tailed hawk perched on a fence post, but very few creatures, feathered or human, stir on this frigid morning.

A curve in the gravel road brightens my face and transforms the drab landscape. I spot an ice-covered pond surging with life, the reward for our early morning journey. Hundreds of trumpeter swans, Canadian geese, and mallards have claimed Beemer's Pond. Before I can pull on my sweatshirt, heavy coat, boots, earmuffs, and scarf, Bill is already heading for the icy water. He is covered from head to foot in winter gear. Only his hazel eyes are visible as he peers through a slit in his facemask, his bare fingers positioned to snap the elusive perfect shot.

Swans, geese, and ducks call to each other, creating a cacophony of sound. The bold, brassy blare of trumpeters directs the high-pitched honking of geese and the nasal quacking of hundreds of mallards. The swans bob in rhythm to an unknown tune. Their graceful movement reminds me of a musician pressing the valves on a French horn.

The performance holds me spellbound. I'm an intruder on a feral orchestra warming up for their morning sonata. The raucous score brims with riotous calls, and the gallantry of outstretched wings rivals any Vegas stage show.

Vigorously led by the trumpet of the swans, the sonata ebbs and flows until the band of feathered musicians stun their audience with sudden flight. The beat of hundreds of wings stills my breath. Bill's camera is clicking. My hands, poised for thunderous applause, rest in midair.

"Encore," I whisper.

WAKING

Essays from
True Words from Real Women

2012

WAKING

Andrea Savee

I LIVED AT THE EDGE OF A WILD GARDEN ONCE, like a stone, cast away. A castaway, stone-cold shoulder turned to the warming weather of the world. But I am no longer immune to the tracings of leaves against my surface, no longer unanswerable to the call of the wind through new openings and over old crevices. From this fitful granite sleep, this disenfranchised grief, I will rally like the red-tailed raptor above me, rising rising rising in the thermals. I will pluck up, endeavor, and dare again to tumble amidst and wrangle with the flowers and the weeds, first with one and then the other. I am willing. I am willing.

DROUGHT AND GRIEF

Susan J. Tweit

You have to get over the color green.
— WALLACE STEGNER

WALLACE STEGNER'S ADVICE ABOUT HOW TO LIVE SUSTAINABLY in the inland West is not a suggestion. You won't survive, he says, in these largely arid expanses between the 100th meridian and the relatively well-watered West Coast, if your soul requires green.

Especially this year; especially in the Southwest and the Southern Rockies, where last winter's snow pack—the source of our summer water—was so sparse as to be scary, and spring heated up so quickly that even that paltry moisture simply vanished.

Which is why in late June, before "normal" fire season began, Colorado had nine wildfires burning, three in the southwestern corner, two west and one east of Colorado Springs, one near Leadville, and two in northern Colorado. The largest two turned out to be the state's most destructive ever, the 83,000-plus acre High Park Fire in the foothills of the Front Range west of Fort Collins, which burned nearly 250 homes and cabins and cost more than $29 million to fight; and the Waldo Canyon Fire, which burned 18,247 acres and 346 homes immediately west of Colorado Springs.

The high temperature here in Salida, Colorado, at 7,000-feet elevation in a mountain valley that is always dry but not usually this parched, topped out at 99°F on June 22. That's the hottest by far in the fifteen years I've lived in this spectacular swath of high desert in the rain-shadow of the tallest stretch of the Rockies.

I feel as tattered and worn as the tiger swallowtail butterfly that lit on the flower basket hanging on my front porch this morning and just clung there as if exhausted, not even moving around to sip nectar from the petunias. That butterfly looked as if it had been through heck and back, its tails and the lower edges of its wings broken off, and the scales completely rubbed away in several places.

The landscapes I love are hurting in this drought, and that hurts me, too. I can water the native grasses and wildflowers in my yard sparingly to keep them alive, but I can't water the mountainsides around my valley. I can only watch helplessly as mountain meadows, usually green at this time of year, turn brown, as the evergreen foliage of the pinyon pines and junipers on the nearby hillsides begins to dull, as the streams and the green band of riparian vegetation they nurture shrink.

We received less than three inches of total precipitation in the first six-plus months of the year. That's not enough to keep alive the living communities that animate these landscapes—from microscopic soil inhabitants to black bears and towering ponderosa pines, from rustling willows to lithe trout. These landscapes have survived long droughts before, including the decades of drought in the late 1100s that were a factor in causing the Ancestral Puebloan people to move from cliff dwellings like those of Mesa Verde to more reliable water sources along the region's major rivers. But I'm guessing that survival wasn't easy, or pretty.

As I watch the landscapes I love wither in this extraordinary drought, I grieve for the losses. For the company we humans are losing as each individual, and in some cases, whole populations of plants and animals, die out. For the homes burned in the wildfires. If this is global climate change, I hate it already.

And I grieve for my personal losses, too, especially that of the love of my life, my husband, sculptor and economist Richard Cabe, he of the brilliant mind and boundless creativity, gone on to whatever is next in the cycle of life, after he died of brain cancer last November.

How do we survive times like this? I know that I turn to nature, be it ever so beleaguered by drought and fire, and look for the grace notes—like that tattered tiger swallowtail or the brilliant Indian paintbrush still blooming in the restored native grassland that serves as my front-yard "unlawn"—signaling that life manages to thrive despite all.

Those small miracles remind me that joy lives on; I only have to pay attention and let it in.

THE THIRD NIGHT

Stephanie Dalley

SO THIS IS THE THIRD NIGHT here alone without him. I thought I had done pretty well, some soul searching, some plan making, lunch with a friend, getting errands done that are long overdue, feeling pleased with those accomplishments.

And here it is the third night home alone, thoughts of this week's upcoming tests and their results worry at the edge of my mind, still it could be a miracle, the one he keeps talking about, the one where the doctor says the whole darn ugly mess is gone, it's missing, maybe we made a mistake? Maybe it was never there? And who am I to doubt the workings of God?

And here it is the third night alone and the damn radio is playing Rod Stewart: *Sometimes when we touch, the honesty's too much . . . I want to hold you till I die, till we both break down and cry, I want to hold you till the fear in me subsides . . .* Please, I think, please don't leave me.

These past two days, the sense of peace I have been so driven to claim, the meditations, the walks, the mindful activities, all look ridiculous now. Mindfulness won't keep you alive, I won't be okay if you leave me. I know I will be just fine, lots of support, friends, family, finances set up, that's not what I am worried about, it's the not talking to you, who else is going to call me from time to time just to say hi? Who else is going to help me figure out what's what, when I can't? *Who else is going to bring me a bottle of rain?* (Thanks, Rod, you seem to have all the right lines tonight).

And then I go away from this room, away from the computer, and I have a deep heartfelt cry, from my gut, from my heart, from my soul, the pent-up pain, feeling so much sorrow and outrage, I think it might swallow me whole.

But it doesn't.

A desperate friend has been texting me, perhaps she is psychic and doesn't even know it; I look at my phone and see the numerous attempts to get my attention. "Are you OK? I have tried several times to reach you, could you please just send me an X if you are OK? Let me know you are there."

I giggle (what else can you do after an emotional storm like that?), send her an X, say a prayer, think of all the good things I have in my life, and come out and finish this piece. Thanks for friends, thanks for every day I've had and will have with him, thanks for the love I experience every day, thanks for writing, thanks for readers. It's good to know you are out there.

MAY I HAVE A WORD WITH YOU?

Mary Ann Parker

WHEN I WRITE, I ROLL A WORD AROUND in my mind as if I am tasting it. Reading a word, speaking a word, hearing a word, or writing a word can be as breathtaking as holding a lovely piece of glass to the light. I delighted in my baby's first word. The first word a child reads for himself brings a sense of accomplishment for him and encouragement from others. Of course, we find meaning as we begin to string words together in thoughts and sentences, and the words used in the craft of storytelling are remarkable tools, but a single word when considered alone can be a source of amazement.

My English teacher in high school loved the word *murmur*. A musical friend's favorite is *alleluia*. Author and world traveler Francis Mayes says that two of her favorite words are linked together: *departure* and *time*. Poet Molly Peacock says she first fell in love with the word *joy* because it had a circle inside! I love the word *lullaby*.

I fell in love with poetry because I love tasting the words and looking at them as light shines through.

NUANCES

Laura Strathman Hulka

I LOST A FRIEND YESTERDAY. With that loss, I became painfully aware of the nuances of our language. *Lost* sounds like I set my friend down like recalcitrant keys and forgot where I put her. *Friend* implies a deeper intimacy than *acquaintance*; we were not intimate, yet so much more than mere head-nodding-as-you-pass-by women. My friend Gloria died. By her own hand.

I can tell you some interesting things about her. She was a divorced Catholic with eight grown children. She was retired from many years as a grocery checker. She loved yard sales and flea markets. She shared my love of books, particularly well-crafted mysteries. She loved her significant other, Bob, with whom she had shared fifteen years. Yet *she* was lost. Somewhere in her life was an inner struggle that I didn't look deeply enough to see. I truly regret that. What went on in those last bitter, lonely hours, before she made the decision to leave her loved ones behind, who are now struggling with guilt and grief? What horrors in her life made her go against her religion, which believes suicide to be a sin, and take her own life? I don't know. I will never know.

I lost another friend recently as well, when my best friend of forty-five years, without discussion or response from me, decided that our friendship no longer served a purpose. Again, the nuances flutter in my face like angry wasps and echo in my head with devastating repeats of past conversations. Friend? For forty-five years we experienced our lives together. Boyfriends, proms, marriages, childbirth, divorces, remarriages, and parental deaths. Laughing, crying, discussing books, religion, politics, family, hobbies. I felt that our friendship, our sisterhood, was so deeply rooted that it would never die but would always be there, sometimes in the background, more often in the forefront, a strong presence to rely on, to share with and enjoy. Where did I miss the signs? What happened to make her so determined to destroy what we had spent decades building and nourishing? I don't know. I will never know.

The last member of my mother's immediate family died recently, at ninety-five. As I lost this last uncle and reminisced with his sons about our parents, I became achingly aware that in this loss, an official torch had been passed. I am now the senior generation. My parents are both gone, lost to me in the physical sense but always present in my mind, a kaleidoscope of memories that often bring a sharp burning to my throat and eyes. Did I appreciate them enough when they were alive? Did we ever really understand one another? My uncle was not a friend, in that I knew almost nothing about him except that he loved ice cream and women, not necessarily in that order. Moreover, although he was family, he was not an intimate part of my life, as were my parents, as are my sisters and my children. Will I ever be able to wrap my head around being a senior citizen, the one family comes to (or groans over) for family stories, pictures, reminiscences, and tall tales? I don't know. I will never know.

Why is it, I wonder, we become increasingly introspective as we age? Why is it, at around age forty, we begin to search for self, for meaning, for a solid grasp on the nebulous thoughts of spirituality, religion, friendship, loss, and family? Why does it matter so much, as we age, that we understand these things, express our beliefs, share our lives, explain our viewpoints, and cherish our loves? Why do the delicate, tremulous nuances of our language both tempt and repel me as I attempt once again to express my thoughts and feelings?

I don't know, and perhaps I will never know. And guess what? That's okay.

DEAR MOMMA

Bea Epstein

DEAR MOMMA,

For many years, my thoughts returned to how unbalanced and unfair I was in my selective memories of the role you played in my life. I realized that for far too long, I saw you through a negative lens. Your life became a model of how not to be a wife and mother. Looking back, I see how much energy I spent proving that I am your total opposite.

Yet, woven through my life has been the hidden recognition that much of what is strongest in me is due to your influence. It wasn't until after you were gone that I could acknowledge this truth. A woman with barely a sixth-grade education, you had little life experience outside the limits of your ghetto world—first in Russia, then in America. How did you know so much about molding a daughter who could, in one generation, take hold of and enjoy the advantages this country has to offer? With no opportunities to realize your own extraordinary potential, where did you learn to think with such shrewdness and complexity?

As your confidante, it was difficult to hear your disappointment in Dad and the dissatisfaction you felt building a life with a naive, unrealistic husband. During those intimate conversations, as I sat and listened without defending him, I was flooded with guilt. No father could have given a daughter more unconditional love and adoration than he gave me.

In our blue-collar immigrant neighborhood, surrounded by working-class families, you let me know in a hundred ways that I had to aspire to something better. With fierce intensity, you believed in my ability to realize your image of the American dream. You pushed, you prodded, you demanded of me an ever-higher level of academic achievement and social grace. No lapse escaped your watchful eye, and your disapproval was all too plain. Launched on this path early in life, I dealt with the intense pressures you placed on me by attaining and even surpassing your expectations.

I always knew it was because of your determination, your energy and drive, that I was able to forge a life so different from your own—a life filled with opportunity, education, and realized potential. In truth, from earliest childhood, I recognized that you were the smartest, most complicated, and most difficult person in my world.

As I grew into the person you groomed me to become, we both felt the distance between us increasing. Asserting my right to be a separate person, I pulled away from you. My comfort in an educational and social class so different from the one in which you lived, combined with my new emotional separateness, wounded you deeply. With less and less to talk about, less and less to share, we grew awkward in each other's presence.

Although I attained precisely the life you desperately struggled to give your children, you saw my gains not as your gains, but as your losses. You were certain we would never be close again and you were so right.

After my marriage, you became increasingly bitter and discouraged with the direction your own life had taken. Dad's debilitating depressions, your continued distance from your son, and my move far from New York added to the loneliness and resentment that formed a shell around you, a shell neither your grandchildren nor I could penetrate.

For years, I struggled to bring some joy into your life. Only after your death was I released from the guilt and shame of every one of our conversations, always hearing the disappointment in your voice. When I no longer felt the need to keep you at bay, I allowed myself to recognize what a remarkable woman you were. Only later in my own life did I understand the traumas you faced as a child and again as a young woman. Only then could I fully appreciate our story as another in the millions of stories of immigrant families who came to America to find a better life for the next generation.

I deeply regret that I was unable to bridge the gap between us before your death more than thirty years ago, so that we might have had the opportunity to forge a closer, more positive connection. I wish I could have separated from you and your disappointment while still honoring you, still acknowledging your profound influence on the best of the woman I became.

Forgive me, Momma. I love you,
Beebee

MAGIC WAND: THE BROOMSTRAWS

Jamuna Advani

JIRIBAM, MANIPUR, INDIA, 1945

I was swinging under the shade of my grapefruit tree when I saw a man approach. Paying no attention to me, he went straight to our house and knocked slowly on the main door. I immediately recognized him as he had visited us before. I called him *Khura*, which meant *uncle*, a sign of respect. When my grandmother opened the door, she looked surprised to see him, then greeted him and signaled him to sit on a *mura* (a stool made of cane) on the veranda, the place where visitors were entertained. He sat down.

"Any problem?" she asked. People from the neighboring villages usually came to my father for help in legal matters.

"Yes, it is to convey news about your son-in-law," he answered.

"What's happened?"

He mumbled something I couldn't hear, then left a few minutes later. I saw grandmother Sanachaobi deep in thought. Then she signaled me to come inside. I jumped off the swing and walked briskly toward her, keen to hear what had just happened. Inside the house I saw her talking to my mother in a very serious tone.

She looked at me and said, "Your father has eloped with Kunjo."

I could not believe it, because Kunjo was a married woman, still living with her husband at the neighboring village Kalinagar. We had heard rumors of their affair but couldn't believe this would happen.

"Where are they now?"

"At Lakhipur, at your Aunt Pashot's place." Lakhipur was a small village, about a ten-mile walk from Jiribam.

Both my mother and grandmother had to accept my father's new wife. Women were not educated and depended mostly on their husbands for living.

Three days later my father returned to attend to his office. His new routine was that on Saturdays he went to his new wife and came back on Sundays. This went on for about a month. He looked exhausted walking ten miles on the hilly dirt road every weekend and it also became a big strain financially, so grandmother suggested building a cottage for Kunjo in space available near our main house. Father immediately started collecting materials for the project and built the house by himself within three months. There was no drainage system, no electricity.

Four months after their elopement, Kunjo was brought to the new cottage. Everything went on normally like a fairy tale, except that Kunjo was not allowed to cook. Being a divorcee and also not from the same caste rank as my grandmother, she was not allowed to enter the kitchen, but she did do other household chores.

My father wanted a son for the family. But Kunjo did not have a child with her previous husband and it was doubtful she could give my father a son.

Another three months had passed when, one day, my grandmother asked me to come inside our main house. Curious, I obeyed. She pulled out a paper from a packet and gave it to me to read. I found it very difficult to understand.

"Read it again carefully to the end. You have to follow the instructions."

I started reading again slowly. I got goose bumps. "No, I don't think I can do it." Someone in the village had given my grandmother the name of a sorcerer, whom she had paid for the mantra I'd just read.

"I am with you, just follow all the instructions," she said. "Only we have to be very careful. No one else should know. Your mother is not a part of this. We are doing this for the welfare of the family."

Reluctantly, I obeyed her. I worked to memorize the mantra written on that piece of paper, which was not easy as the words were an ancient language used by our ancestors.

Three days later, we saw Kunjo all dressed up, a Champa flower hanging on the left side from her hair, which gave a heavenly scent. She said she had to go to Kali temple and also meet her friend. Once she was out of the gate and walked on the street toward Kali temple, my grandmother, who was at the loom weaving, immediately came out to see if Kunjo was far enough for us to proceed with our plan. She signaled me to go into Kunjo's bedroom.

Once inside, I saw that the room was neatly arranged and filled with the sweet fragrance of Champa flowers, which Kunjo kept near her bed. I took a deep breath as my heart started pumping faster. Even though it was safe to follow the instructions, I was still scared.

Slowly I pulled out five pieces of broomstraw from the packet and, holding them in my right hand, I recited the mantra three times on those broomstraws. Then I continued, sweeping the broomstraws on her bed from the middle toward the opposite sides. After repeating this three times I left the room as fast as I could with the packet. My grandmother's face was still turned toward the road watching for Kunjo. She was relieved when she saw me.

For four months we continued the same ritual regularly. Then, something, we weren't sure what, happened between Kunjo and my father. One fine morning she left for her parent's home in Cachar and never returned. Father did not mention her again.

I still wonder if that magic wand worked, or if it was another reason. Now that Kunjo was gone, I heard my grandmother asking her friends to find a young bride for my father. A son was needed for the family's name to continue.

AN AFTERNOON
WITH MR. MORGAN

Helen (Len) Leatherwood

MR. MORGAN WAS A RETIRED EPISCOPAL PRIEST who lived a few houses up from my family on East Ninth Street in my hometown of Bonham, Texas. He and his wife, Anna, must have been in their mid-seventies when I was young. They both had white hair, and they walked with the stoop that comes with advanced age.

Mr. Morgan had an office on one end of his house, with a private entrance. When I was five or six, I often visited him there, and when I arrived, he'd open a large closet where he had several games stored. He would allow me to pick the game I wanted, and then he and I would proceed to play either checkers or chess or my very favorite: pick-up sticks.

For the game of pick-up sticks, we'd settle on the floor of the office. I don't remember any difficulty Mr. Morgan had sitting on the floor, though now I can imagine it was a good deal more difficult for him than for me. Once we were situated on the rug, Mr. Morgan would put the pile of brightly colored sticks on their ends. In anticipation, I would wait for the moment when he released them and they fell in a tangled jumble on the floor. The object of the game was to carefully remove one stick at a time without disturbing any of the other sticks. Mr. Morgan and I spent lots of time carefully teasing out those red, green, and yellow sticks from the pile, each taking a turn when the other caused a slight wiggle. I remember his hand, liver-spotted and pale white, deftly manipulating those little sticks. He might have been old, but his hand was completely steady and he was a formidable opponent. Sometimes I won; sometimes he won. I appreciated that Mr. Morgan never let me win. He was a real opponent.

While he and I were playing the game I had chosen for that day, Mrs. Morgan would always come in at some point and say hello. Then she would disappear for a few minutes, only to reappear with a plate of cookies and lemonade. Mr. Morgan and I would continue to play while we munched on the cookies. We were serious about our games so we didn't stop just to eat.

I had fun playing games with Mr. Morgan. I looked forward to my impromptu visits, and from his smile I knew he was happy to see me. He was always dressed in a suit when I visited, no matter whether it was morning or afternoon, and Mrs. Morgan always had on a dress, never slacks or even a skirt. They were good and proper people, I knew even at my young age, and very decent indeed.

I would announce at home that I was going over to play with Mr. Morgan and my parents would just smile and say, "Have fun."

I did and he did and we did and even now I think of that nice old man sitting in his office with its roll-top desk, walls covered with filled-to-the-brim bookshelves, that closet with its shelf of games, and the floor where he and I sat and carefully and strategically dislodged stick after stick during our pick-up sticks game. This remains one of the loveliest images of my childhood: an old man, a young girl, and an afternoon with nothing more to do than to sit on the floor and play a game. What could be more perfect? Or more special?

THE FACE IN THE MIRROR

Joyce Boatright

IN THE SUMMER OF 1960, right before I entered high school, my daddy dyed my hair red. Yep, that's right. He put on those rubber gloves and mixed the color with peroxide and then, with my head hanging over the bathroom sink, he painted my wren-brown hair with Miss Clairol's patented Coppertone. My daddy said I was an Irish girl and should have been born a redhead—he was just helping Mother Nature correct her mistake. Wow, what a difference! My hair dazzled.

There were lots of blondes, a passel of brunettes, and a few chestnut-haired girls in high school, but I have to say, in all honesty and with a smidgen of humility, that I was the only redhead worth noticing.

I wasn't beautiful, but I've always been pretty. While my girlfriends fought acne, I had a peaches-and-cream complexion that came from good genes rather than any kind of skin regimen. At five-foot-four and a hundred and sixteen pounds, I had the curves of Marilyn Monroe. I remember that my favorite lipstick was Pink Parfait, which I bought at Goolsby Drugstore on the Courthouse Square of my hometown.

My mother tried her best to interest me in the latest fashion from New York, but I was more interested in the fads of my age group. I wanted to fit in, not stand out. Except for the red hair, that is. I did like that bodacious red hair—mainly because my daddy kept telling me how pretty I was, and my Aunt Jean went out and bought the same Miss Clairol and colored her hair right after she saw mine. I knew I had to be good-looking if my aunt wanted to copy me.

That red hair laid the foundation for a girl who combined sassy with savvy. I gained confidence that my mental prowess could make up for my less-than-Miss-Texas beauty-queen looks with each degree I earned: high school diploma, bachelor's degree in journalism and English, master's degree in educational administration with a specialty in public relations, and a doctorate in adult education with a specialty in higher education marketing.

At twenty-five, I had spurned five marriage proposals and then succumbed to a man who proposed to me four months into our relationship. I said yes. I wouldn't say it was love at first sight or a whirlwind courtship. Actually—and I know this is hard to believe but it's true—in some quirky six-degrees turn of fate, my mother had been flower girl in his parents' wedding. Because of that little detail, we decided that even though we hadn't known each other very long, we were well matched. Good stock. Crazy about each other. And we wanted to be married like our friends were. What else was necessary? We had the rest of our lives to get to know each other. I was, after all, twenty-five years old and not getting any younger.

The marriage lasted four years, seven months, and twenty-five days. By then the hard reality of spending a lifetime together had sullied all illusions of wedded bliss. What we knew of each other wasn't strong enough to hold us together until our fifth anniversary, much less the rest of our lives.

My thirties were the most powerful of my young existence—I was smart, I was pretty, and men and women listened when I voiced my ideas.

Then I became middle-aged. My youth faded and my body began to betray me. I had a hysterectomy and gained twenty pounds, began taking steroids for ulcerative colitis and gained another thirty pounds. I've been fighting—and sometimes winning—the battle of body image ever since.

This morning, I take a look in the mirror and see my reflection. All else has been stripped away—the lipstick, the silky smooth skin, the husband. Even the red hair is fading to gray. I face who I really am. It has taken time—and faded youth—to see *me*. Not someone else's idea of me, but truly *me*. And I like her.

But there's no need to toss Miss Clairol out the window. Instead, I've chosen to fade to honey blonde. After all, the aging soul needs to glow.

UGLY DUCKLING
TO HOWLING WOLF

Rhonda Wiley-Jones

I WAS DROPPED BY THE STORK on the wrong doorstep, a daughter and later a sister in a strange place—in a place where I often felt out of place. Mother and Daddy read folktales to us from the *Book of Knowledge Encyclopedia* that crowned the bookcase headboard in their bedroom. They read my favorite, "The Ugly Duckling," to me so many times they had it memorized and soon I was "reading" it to my younger brothers from memory. I was decades old before I looked in my pond to see my reflection and saw a swan's grace.

I was never trouble. I was a good girl. I stole a role and made it fit, then decided to make it my own. I played my script from the cards dealt to me. I functioned in apprehension, afraid of being found out. But I was never trouble.

I lived with an itch just beneath the surface. I felt ground down sometimes, disconnected from the place I called home and the people who were my community. Over time I was born again and again and again until I was plumb pagan in their eyes. But I was never trouble.

Today I move quietly into the world, fresh, redeemed, and reborn with a passport in hand that ensures my travel to other landscapes and places, people, and cultures. I reclaim my birthright to become the disruptive creative force I was meant to be. It's time I become trouble.

Clarissa Pinkola Estes in *Women Who Run with the Wolves* reminds women to run with the wildness within them. Natalie Goldberg challenges women to write hot and deep and wild and crazy, while Allen Ginsberg shows us how to rail against the injustices of life in his poem, "Howl." They each call forth that place where we are natural and nurtured, but wild.

That natural core is where I find that I alone exist, uniquely me, bound by nothing but the primordial essence of God, Mother Earth, Spirit Wind.

I learn to dash naked through the virgin forest to howl at the moon. To dance on the Wind, skirt the Stars, and land on Mars, all in the twinkle of an eye. To imagine the world before it was breathed into being. To move the world with the ease of Atlas. To write deeply because the whole of the universe resides in me.

I grasp the call to howl when others have denied God ever existed, to let them know He is still there for them. To howl when a child fades in a mother's arms because love does not feed the little belly. To howl when some take the truth and twist it until they recreate the facts, spinning logic on its heels. I howl when *one nation under God* is torn asunder because we don't believe in *with liberty and justice for all.* To howl when I realize I am a stranger in my own family. To howl when life bears down and I must beg for strength to soldier on. And to howl when I put myself into the world with the joy and fear of being exposed each time I put words to paper.

It's time I become trouble.

As threads of insight appear over the years, slowly evolving, I collect them in journals on the shelf, in boxes stowed beneath the bed, and in crevices in my mind. I weave them together on the warp of my life to construct the fabric of a re-created self. I join the scribe inside me to set down my tales of exploitations in the world. When and as I do, the spirits of far-away places greet me. What have seemed to be random experiences become a tapestry. With each escapade I create something rich and full and beautiful.

The chronicling of my journeys carries forth lessons I garnered along the way on a universal scale—for me, for anyone called by the spirit of adventure to leave home. At each sojourn's end, I reminisce with treasures, memories, or souvenirs. The first treasure is always the *story*, evidence of where I've been.

I bring myself home evolved to live among those that remained at home to garner their own lessons close at hand. I forgive them their indifference, those who stayed behind either unable or unwilling to trek to parts unknown.

This is why I sally forth into the world, not with a goal in mind, but a purpose to discover the unknown. In the discovery is the surprise for which my soul yearns; but the journey is requisite for me to own the lesson. Had I ignored the seductive summons and remained at home, the swan would have remained a secret and the wolf silent.

RECOGNIZING

Essays from
True Words from Real Women

2013

THE LITTLE GIRL
IN THE PHOTOGRAPH

Pat Bean

I WAS IN MY SEVENTIES when a cousin sent me a small black-and-white photo that changed the whole context of my childhood. I knew the picture was me only because of its back inscription: Patricia Lee Joseph, age three.

The little girl's pale, straw-colored hair was curled into neatly arranged ringlets, the short, puffed-sleeved frock she wore had clearly been starched and pressed to perfection, and beneath her black patent leather Mary Janes, she wore lace-trimmed socks.

This was not the childhood I remembered. I remembered one in which I went to school with straight, tangled hair and hand-me-down clothes. Together with my bratty know-it-all nature, which was reflected even in the scowl on the face of the daintily dressed little girl in the photo, I came to be called cootie-brain by jeering classmates. It was a name that stuck with me all the way through the end of fifth grade, which was the year my grandmother died and we were forced to move from her home.

I blamed my mother for both my unhappiness and our family's dysfunctional nature. She was always grouchy and unpleasant. And when my dad came home at night, usually long after I had been put to bed, she was especially angry with him. I would put the pillow over my head to block out the bitter words she screeched, but my mother had a sharp and penetrating voice, and the small cushion was a weak defense.

I was in my mid-thirties before the reality that my mother had good reason to be angry hit me, like Thor's hammer coming down on a dimwitted skull. But then children don't see the world through the same eyes as those of an adult, and I had still been a child when I married at barely sixteen to escape the discord.

My day of recognition was the one on which I sat, unweeping, at my father's sparsely attended funeral. For the first time, I suddenly knew that my mother had cause to be angry at my always cheerful, but seldom present, father. His early demise at fifty-five, I realized, was probably hastened by his alcoholism, for an alcoholic is what he was, and a gambler as well.

The words of those midnight sessions my mother had with my father, which were especially frightful on Friday nights, replayed themselves in my mind. Sitting at his funeral, I realized my father hadn't come home until he had gambled and drunk away most, or all, of his weekly paycheck.

He was the reason I wore hand-me-downs and sometimes went to school with holes in my shoes. He was the reason I had been forced to go out in the neighborhood to sell my mother's beautiful crocheting. It was that money, I now realized, that had helped put food on our table. I also remembered the many times when my father, who drove the family car, failed to pick me up as he had promised so I could attend a school event.

I had forgotten all these things, and overlooked them when I was a child, because in person, my dad was always kind and funny and cheerful, everything my mother was not.

I eventually reconciled with my mother, coming to appreciate her many strengths, and realizing that the year I had started first grade, she had given birth to her second child, and then a third one less than a year later. At the same time, she had planted a huge garden every year, canned its bounty, and dutifully taken care of my bedridden grandmother.

While my mother's personality could at times be abrasive, and she was not much of a hugger, her love for us children was real. She expressed it by making sure we had a roof over our heads and a hot-cooked meal on the table every evening.

Even accepting this reality, there was still a lingering small voice that whispered in my ear, telling me that my mother never loved me. Why else would she have allowed me to go to school with my hair looking like it actually had cooties, as my peers had claimed? Yet here was proof, in a tiny black-and-white photo of a girl with ringlets in her hair, that she did love me.

I was surprised to receive the photograph, because the same year I had started a new school in sixth grade, I had gathered up all the photos of myself and burned them. I had been determined to put my past behind me and start fresh, and the ugly photos of me, with my stringy hair, skinny body, and freckled face, were part of that past. I had no choice but to destroy them.

I realized that the only way this one small picture of me had survived was because it had been taken by my aunt, my mother's older sister. Looking at it also brought back another memory that I had long suppressed. It was of me, the first day of school, sitting on a stool with my mother trying to tame my tangled, unruly hair.

The bratty kid I was back then screamed and yelled and cried that she was hurting me. Maybe she was, but I'm sure not as much as I pretended. With the picture of the little girl in ringlets still in my hand, I reheard the words my mother finally uttered that same morning.

"Well, from now on, you can comb your hair yourself," she said. Then she put down the comb and walked away, never again to touch my hair.

My going to school with uncombed hair had nothing to do with love. It was all about my mother being a woman who, unlike my dad, stood by her words.

A Child's Sorrow

Kim Heikkila

VALENTINE'S DAY, SATURDAY, FEBRUARY 14, 2009

The day starts with some light snow showers. Steve is running late, so I leave for the church alone, without him and Tu. I arrive early and wait in the parking lot for ten minutes, watching them bring Mom's coffin in from the funeral coach. Steve and Tu arrive after I've gone inside.

We sit in the front row of the nave, Mom's small clan of progeny: the three of us and Eric. Swells of music from the giant pipe organ fill the church but leave me cold. The pastor reads the biography of Mom I wrote. It ends with her own words about love: "Love gives us companions to find our way through this world with, though our gait be uneven and our music out of tune."

Tu is quiet for most of the service, but at one point begins whispering, "Dead, died, dying, dead dead dead."

Eric rides with us to the cemetery. Tu falls asleep. We leave Tu in the car as a small crowd gathers around the grave just a few steps away. Steve retrieves him when he begins to rustle. They join us as an awkward silence descends after the pastor finishes speaking. Eric gets things moving by putting his stalk of wheat on our mother's coffin. I save mine.

We leave Mom behind, in her coffin, hovering over a hole in the cold, February ground. Eric, Steve, Tu and I have dinner at Perkins. The waitress gives us a heart-shaped cookie.

"Can I have that?" Tu asks.

"Yes," I say.

Good-bye, Mom.

WANDERINGS, FRIDAY, FEBRUARY 20, 2009

Today Tu and I go to a sing-a-thon at a local high school, a fundraiser for an organization that provides financial assistance for families affected by cancer. We sit in the middle of the auditorium in the middle of a school day to listen to teenagers sing. At one point, Tu pulls out his toy phone and calls Grandma so she can listen to the music because, he says, "it will be beautiful."

One of the student-singers dedicates her song to her mother, who has been diagnosed with pancreatic cancer.

"She's going to die," I imagine saying to the girl. "She's going to die, she's going to die, she's going to die . . ." I can't even dream up any platitudes, any hopeful words. "She's going to die."

But I also think, *It could be worse. I could be in high school.*

ONE WEEK, SATURDAY, FEBRUARY 21,2009

I check on Mom's empty house today, shovel the newly fallen snow. I take pictures of the house to preserve something of it after it's sold. Tu and Steve come over later. It's the first time Tu has been here since Grandma has not.

"Is Grandma upstairs?" he asks.

"No," I reply. "Remember what happened to Grandma?"

"She died. Can I go upstairs?"

I let him go. When he returns, he asks where Grandma is.

"She's resting," I say.

"No. Where did she go?"

I pause, not knowing what he wants.

"Where did she go? She was in that big box. Where did she go?"

It dawns on me what his three-year-old mind needs to know.

"She went into the ground. They put that box in the ground and buried her."

He's satisfied.

Grammaphone, Thursday, February 26, 2009

Tu calls Grandma again on his purple plastic phone. He says she wants to talk to me. I tell her I have a headache today. She says to take medicine and drink water. I hand the phone back to Tu, and he carries on his half of a conversation. He says Grandma doesn't feel very good today, that she needs medicine and water.

This purple phone has become Tu's link to Grandma. He has a Grammaphone.

Peeps, Monday, March 2, 2009

It's the Peeps that get me this morning.

I stop in the middle of the Easter candy aisle at Rainbow and stare at the sugar-coated marshmallow bunnies. I shut my eyes and let loose a silent scream. *Aaaaauuuggghhhh.* Mom loved Peeps. She gave us Peeps every Easter, including last year, when I was almost forty years old.

I don't even like them, but I put several boxes of Peeps in my cart. For Tu.

Later, Tu and I watch television. Cartoon bunnies, Max and Ruby, tussle over buying birthday presents for Grandma. I want to chuck the remote at the television. Instead, I reach for the Peeps.

"Have a Peep, Tu."

"Can I have two?"

"How about three?"

We watch the rest of the program with yellow sugar sticking to our fingers and teeth.

LEAVE-TAKING, MONDAY, MARCH 16, 2009

Tu and I go to the cemetery today. It's a beautiful day—65 degrees and sunny. By the time we arrive, Tu has fallen asleep, so I leave him in the car.

I walk around by myself, enjoying the silence and the sun. I return to the car, intending to leave, but can't quite do it. I stare at Mom's grave, easy to spot on the otherwise uniform lawn.

By now, Tu is awake. I take him out to see Grandma's grave, show him her name on the headstone, introduce him to the Grandpa he never knew.

"Can I sit on that?" he asks, pointing to the tilted headstone.

"Yes," I say, knowing Mom would like it.

"Too bad we can't see Grandma."

There are a few wheat stalks still near the site. Tu and I pick some up and write a message to Mom in the wet sand.

Hi, Mom! Hi, Grandma! From Tu. 3/16/09

I suggest we leave, but Tu needs more time.

"Not yet. I want to sit here and look at the dirt." He pauses. "Grandma's still buried there."

When finally we pull away, we say, "Bye, guys! See you soon."

Tu adds, "When you're alive again."

BARBIE DOLL

Juliana Lightle

BARBARA LEWIS DUKE, PRETTY, PETITE, BLUE-EYED AND BLOND, my mother, one fearless, controlling woman. Long after Mom's death, Dad said, "Barbara was afraid of absolutely no one and nothing!"

They married late: thirty-four and thirty-eight. He adored her unconditionally. She filled my life with horses, music, love, cornfields, hayrides, books, and ambition. Whatever she felt she had missed, my sister and I were going to possess: books, piano lessons, a college education. Her father, who died long before I was born, loved fancy, fast horses. So did she. During my pre-school, croupy years, she quieted my hysterical night coughing with stories of runaway horses pulling her in a wagon. With less than one hundred pounds and lots of determination, she stopped them, a tiny Barbie doll flying across the Missouri River Bottom, strong, willful, and free.

TRIPPING AROUND JOHN'S BARN

Judy Sheer Watters

MOM IS NINETY-TWO YEARS YOUNG. I really love my mom, but sometimes her thought process makes me want to tear out my hair. Oh, don't get me wrong. Mom is definitely in charge of all her mental faculties. She can remember everything in her youth, all the birthdays of her relatives, and even what kind of bagel she had for breakfast. However, sometimes discussing everyday matters will take the two of us around John's barn.

John's barn? "Who's John?" you ask. Going around John's barn is an expression I remember Mom using from the time I was very young. No one knows John; it just means going in circles in our conversations. Let me give you an example.

For many years, Mom and I have quilted together, making blankets for children, grandchildren, and great-grandchildren. Five years ago, Mom's arthritic hands stopped holding a needle altogether, so she continued to sew blankets by osmosis—meaning, I cut the pieces out; I sewed the pieces together; I put the binding on the blanket; Mom presented the blanket to a loved one. Recently, my fingers also have given in to arthritis.

"Mom," I said one day, "a friend of mine told me about the Quilt House. You take a two-hour class for $35.00 and then you can use their quilting machine to finish out the blanket for just $15.00 an hour. That would be so much easier on my hands. What do you think?"

Being the frugal lady that she has always been, Mom said, "Then you have to add the cost of batting."

"Well, that's right, Mom," I said. "You take in the finished top and the backing, along with the batting to go in between. Or you can purchase the batting at their shop."

"That's what I thought," Mom said with a *humph*. "You have to buy the batting from them."

I tried again. "No, Mom, you can bring your own batting if you prefer."

"But you still have to buy the batting," she insisted.

"Mom, we always have to buy batting for the filler. We would have to buy it even if we didn't use the machine at the Quilt House."

"And there you have it."

"Have what?" I asked.

"You have to buy the batting," Mom said without missing a beat.

It was at this point that I wondered what color John had painted his barn this year. I remember in my youth making countless trips around his barn with Mom. I thought I should try one more time. "Mom, walk through this with me. You and I cut out small pieces and then sew them together to form a blanket top, right?"

"Yes," she agreed.

"Then we find backing from all your fabric, and we match the two pieces up, then slide the batting in between for a fluffy blanket, right?"

"Right." She was still marching in time with me.

"Where do we usually get that batting?"

"Walmart." Still with me.

"Mom, the only difference in going to the Quilt House is that they have a huge machine to run the layers through to be quilted."

"And we have to buy the batting," Mom reminded me.

My sister, Virginia, walked in at that time and immediately recognized that look on my face. She knew that Mom and I just had another glorious trip around John's barn.

But that's not the end of this story. As I drove home that day, I reflected on John's barn. Having grown up on a farm in Pennsylvania, I think of a barn with a nostalgic sense of well-being, of home. It's a warm feeling of security. My mother gives me this same safe-and-sound down-home blessing every time I am in her presence. She has given me years of unconditional love and unremitting joy.

I look forward to experiencing many more delightful trips around John's barn with my precious mom.

MY DAUGHTER'S BABY

Jane Louise Steig Parsons

AS MY FOURTEEN-YEAR-OLD DAUGHTER SITS ON A CHAIR in our back yard practicing the French horn, I notice that her beloved baby possum is at home upon her shoulder. As is his custom, the tiny possum is using all four hands to steady himself on his lofty perch. He lifts his overly large head to sniff the morning air and contentedly peers into his world through inquisitive, bright eyes.

What a gift this baby possum is to her—so responsive, so affectionate—despite his genetic wildness. An orphan, thwarted by his blood mother's absence, he is compelled to seek the warmth of maternal closeness. Through his attention and touch he is training his adopted mother to treasure their unlikely intimacy.

In response to the silky face he presses against her cheek, my daughter stops practicing her horn and silently studies her small charge. In disbelief, she watches her baby possum lean forward, neck extended, and slowly, carefully, place his sensitive, pale pink nose into the silver mouthpiece. A proud, radiant smile forms upon my daughter's lips as she muses in the way of all mothers, and whispers, "He wants to be just like me!"

I feel truly blessed as I witness this heart-warming relationship within our family. As time passes, I continue to watch in awe as my daughter and her adopted baby share the affection and gentleness of this exquisite bonding between a young human and a young mammal, each rejoicing in the other's friendship and touch.

It is now many years since I was privileged to observe this remarkable adventure our family shared. Even today, when I sit quietly and close my eyes, I, too, feel our baby possum's touch and a gentle warmth fills my heart.

THE VACATION

Susan Lines

I REMEMBER A VACATION WE TOOK—my parents, my brother, and I—back in the mid-1950s. It was to Long Beach, Vancouver Island, British Columbia, Canada. It was one of two vacations we took while my father was still alive. The plan was that my mother would take us up there for the first week, and my father would arrive for the second week.

This was before the road was put in, now allowing the zillions of tourists who come every year, all year long. In the summer, this beautiful, long sandy beach boasts wonderful beachcombing, sunbathing, rock fishing, and surfing, among others. The winter caters to the storm watchers.

We left Port Alberni on a small freighter called the *Uchuck*. Not much later on, she was replaced by another small freighter named *The Lady Rose*. The trip itself, down the inlet and around to Ucluelet on the west coast of the island, was exciting. We would stop and give groceries and mail to those who would row out and collect their booty.

When we arrived in the little town, we caught an old dusty school bus, which took us out to Long Beach. There, waiting for us, was a small donkey named Dolly, who had the unenviable job of pulling a small cart with luggage, groceries, etc. Her driver was a First Nations elder named Joe.

Down the beach we went, to Peg Whittington's camp, Singing Sands (and the sands did sing). There were about six cabins nestled in the woods. These cabins had been built and used by the Canadian Air Force during World War II. They were stationed there just in case the Japanese attacked. This idea was extremely unlikely, so I would think those boys spent a frustrating time in the isolation, away from the action.

When we arrived at the beach, amid clouds of dust from the gravel road and the wind from the sea, we could hear the boom and crash of the waves on the sand. This seemed to awaken a primal feeling within me, causing me to run and scream, with arms waving wildly, dancing along the edge of the ice cold water. The day was hot, and this activity caused lots of knowing nods and laughter. I seemed to lose all sense of control when I saw and heard those waves thundering in, along with the screaming of the gulls and the smell of the beautiful dark blue-green sea.

Little Dolly obligingly pulled the luggage while we walked almost a mile along the beach to the cabins. Joe helped us with our luggage and groceries, and we quickly settled in. In quick order, it soon became home. We slept like the drift logs on the beach.

The next morning, we started the wonderful explorations of the beach and the surrounding rock outlets with their blowholes, running along the masses of old bleached drift logs that had been storm-tossed high up on the beach. There were glass fishing-floats to be found, and Dungeness crabs in the tidal pools. We found the skeletal remains of a wolf eel one misty morning, very ugly, with wolfish head and teeth and a long snake-like body. Even now, the thought gives me the shivers.

We spent an idyllic week, the weather was beautiful, the cabin ideal, and the beach an indescribable collection of adventures.

Then my father arrived.

He, on the other hand, did not care for this sort of thing. He had begged off coming with us to begin with, saying there was work to do. Upon arriving for the second week, he had trouble walking in the sand, due to his bad leg. So poor little Dolly had to pull him along in the cart. That intensified his very bad mood and the little silver flask soon appeared. If I remember correctly, there were plenty of refills in the suitcase, as we could hear gurgling. Things went from bad to worse, and we left a couple of days later. We may even have been told to leave, I don't recall.

In defense of my father, who was a very unhappy individual and who, unfortunately, would take it out on those he loved, I am sure he did love us as much as he was capable. He had come from a loveless family and was called a cripple. He was always aware of this.

At fifteen, he had contracted polio and lost the use of his left leg. In those days, there were many bullies (even in his family) and lots of taunting. Nothing was ever done, and so, psychologically, he didn't survive. Others might have, but he didn't.

I am sorry that he was not strong enough, as an adult, to overcome these feelings for the sake of his family. Instead he treated us as he had been treated, with coldness, and also used corporal punishment as the method to retain control. I think that in those days (seventy years ago), this was not recognized as being so damaging for the family, especially the children.

Even so, I still remember that first week with such joy. It was perfect happiness.

THE RIGHT THING?

Sheila McNaughton

THE STREETS WERE SLUSHY. Dirty snow piled at the curbs. Lights were on in many homes as I drove through the neighborhood. After a few wrong turns, I found the church and pulled into the empty parking lot. The rectory was dark except for a bulb burning in the frosted globe by the door. I got out of my old blue Maverick and locked it. Shivering, I stuck my hands in the pockets of my long coat and walked up the sidewalk. Should I knock or ring the bell? My tentative raps on the ornate wooden door didn't produce any results so I pushed the button and stepped back as loud chimes rang deep in the house.

A light came on in the foyer, shining through the beveled glass panels beside the door. A young priest in black pants, black shirt, clerical collar, and shiny black shoes opened the door. His light blue eyes and warm smile welcomed me as he held out his hand.

"Hi, Sheila. I'm Father Mike. Come in. We'll go to the sitting room. Let me take your coat." He helped me off with the coat, hanging it and my scarf on a wooden coat rack.

"Can I get you a cup of coffee or tea?"

"No, thanks." I managed to whisper.

He led me down the hall into a dark paneled room lined with books. We sat in green wingback chairs near the brick fireplace with logs crackling. Above the fireplace was a painting of an older priest sitting behind an intricately carved desk. The same desk sat in front of a large window with the tapestry drapes pulled back. The yard was dark and the room was an odd reflection in the glass.

"I spoke to Father Jim at Annunciation Church. He told me you want to talk about Christine and Tom," said Father Mike.

"I don't want to cause trouble for anyone." Looking down at my hands, I remembered the pear-shaped diamond and slender wedding band I had worn three years ago. "Christine is planning to marry Tom in this church in three months. She needs to know about him before she does."

"Have you spoken to her?"

I couldn't look at him, just rubbed the spot where my rings used to be. "No. I don't know what to say."

"Tell me," he said.

"I married Tom and I didn't know. No one knew or if they did, they didn't say."

"What didn't they say?"

I hesitated, not sure I could speak the words aloud. "Tom is gay. He told me he doesn't like women. Why would he do this again?"

"Maybe you should talk to Christine? Or Tom?"

"I can't live through it again. But she has a right to know." I sat closer to the edge of the chair, wiping sweaty palms on my jeans.

"Tell me what happened," he said leaning forward.

My speech had been rehearsed in my head on the ride here. But now unable to speak, tears filled my eyes.

"Here's a tissue," said Father Mike.

Wiping away tears, I raised my eyes to meet his. "We were married in August, 1973. My perfect wedding. Mom made my dress. Everyone was there. My brother came from Florida. My little sister was a bridesmaid. Daddy walked me down the aisle. Tom's family came from all over. Our friends were there. His Lutheran minister was part of the ceremony." I stopped talking as the memories of that day whirled in my head.

"Are you alright? Do you want something to drink?"

"No. I'm okay. Remembering is hard."

"Take your time," he said, sitting back in the chair and crossing his legs.

Looking into the fire, I took a deep breath. "Three months after we were married, I came home from work and found Tom sitting alone in the darkened living room, a bottle of scotch on the table beside him. He didn't say hello, just sat slumped in the chair with the glass in his hand. He didn't look at me as he said, 'It isn't personal. I don't like women. I can't be married to you anymore.'"

"He told me to leave, go home to my parents. I did. Ten months later the marriage was legally annulled. I stood before a judge and swore to tell the truth. I said it was because I wanted children and Tom didn't. That was a lie. I couldn't say Tom was gay."

"What do you want me to do?" Father Mike asked.

"Tell her."

We talked a bit more. Father Mike tried to comfort me by saying I had done the right thing. I wanted go home and not think about this ever again.

As he walked me to the door and helped me with my coat, Father Mike promised to take care of things. I unlocked my car and looked back at the rectory. He stood on the porch watching me. I couldn't see his face, only his outline against the light. He stayed there until I turned onto the street. Gripping the steering wheel and watching the road through tears, I prayed I had done the right thing.

Father Mike told Christine on Friday night. She confronted Tom on Saturday morning and broke off the engagement. I heard Tom had been in a rage. Drinking, screaming at his parents, swearing at his brother. He threatened to ruin me as I had ruined him.

Tuesday morning, I stood in the kitchen looking out the window above the sink, grateful for the first sunny day in weeks. I finished my first cup of coffee. Reaching for the pot, I poured another as the wall phone rang. Picking up the receiver I answered, "Hello."

There was no response. "Who is this?"

"Sheila, I'm so sorry to be the one to call." My older brother Shawn spoke in a voice so quiet I almost didn't recognize him. "Tom is dead. He hung himself."

LUCKY DOG

Sallie Moffit

I DIDN'T WANT ANOTHER DOG. I had recently put my beloved pet of twelve years to sleep, and I wasn't ready for a new one. But my husband liked her. He named her Franny, after his cherished grandmother, Frances. A friend told me that when a dog chooses to live at your house, it means the dog will bring you good luck.

The day she wandered into our yard, all I could see the German shepherd bringing us was misery. Her rib bones poked through her pale black fur. Her teats hung down under her belly, flabby from being over-nursed and underfed.

Someone had abandoned the year-and-a-half-old pup in the thick woods of red oaks, hackberries, and mountain cedars near my home. It happens quite often, and I usually call animal control to pick up the stray. But this dog was different. She had been abused.

The cream-colored canine kept her bushy tail tucked firmly between her legs. Fear and distrust were visible in her brown almond-shaped eyes. One day I got her into a dog carrier and tried to pet her. She lowered her head and acted like an invisible whip was beating her. As the gentle dog trembled from my touch, I began to cry. Her wounded soul crumbled the wall guarding my heart, so I decided to give her a chance.

However, when I came near her, she ran. When I fed her, she cowered behind a stack of firewood and wouldn't come out until I left. When I grabbed a leash off the hook on the back porch, she darted away, hiding in the shrubbery lining the embankment along the creek behind our house. Eventually she'd slink back into the yard after I'd gone inside.

The shallow creek behind our house has a limestone bottom that allows many animals, such as coyotes and bobcats, to travel up and down it. Sometimes they venture into our yard. Franny surprised many of them with her deep bark and natural instinct to protect her boundaries. She chased them out of the yard and back into the creek. The smart dog seemed to enjoy patrolling the woods around our house, trotting through the yard with her tail wagging, head held high, tongue hanging out of the side of her mouth. By keeping the wild animals out of our yard, she provided a safe haven for our two cats.

Before long, the curious and playful dog had made remarkable progress. She learned to fetch balls, go for walks, and eat while I was still outside.

Late one summer afternoon, I was in the kitchen preparing dinner when I heard Franny bark. I glanced out the kitchen window and saw her in the back part of the yard. She appeared to have cornered a raccoon or possum and was barking at it.

I marched outside to rescue the scared animal. I scoured the dense mass of gray dogwood and prairie sumac, but I didn't see anything. Franny continued to bark and growl, her black wedge-shaped muzzle sniffing the air. Suddenly, she turned and bolted across the yard, her pointed ears lying flat against her head as her long graceful legs galloped toward the front of the house. I hurried after her. When I passed the corner of the house, I saw Franny charging across the yard, nipping the heels of a man in a red shirt. The man sprinted through the grass trying to outrun the scissor-like jaws of my dog. He seemed to be searching for a break in the vegetation so he could escape into the creek.

I screamed for him to stop. He ignored me, so I yelled again. Franny came to my side, barking fiercely. The man stopped, his short brown hair plastered to his red, sweaty face. While he gasped for air, he explained that he was lost and trying to get down to the creek so he could cross over to a subdivision on the other side. I told him that he was on private property and that he was trespassing. I demanded he get off my property and pointed to the road. My loyal shepherd moved closer to me and growled, baring her teeth.

The man looked around. His options were limited by the thick shrubbery growing near the creek. He had two choices: he could go to the road or go through me and Franny.

I pointed to the chipped-rock lane. "Get off my property now!"

Franny leaned forward, her bushy tail straight behind her, and snarled.

The intruder chose the road.

Once he reached the one lane street, he started running. Within seconds, a police car sped past us and stopped. The officer jumped out with a rifle in his hands and ordered the man to get down on the ground. Franny and I watched while the officer handcuffed and arrested the man in the red shirt.

Later, I discovered the man had broken into a house down the road from me. The homeowner had called the police, and the officer had been in pursuit of the suspect until he disappeared.

Someone asked me if I was scared when I confronted the criminal on my property. After thinking about it for a moment, I said no. I had Franny by my side. And then I realized that even an abused stray can become lucky—with a little love.

ACTING

Essays from
True Words from Real Women

2014

WILD LAVENDER

Linda M. Hasselstrom

The best politics is right action.
— Mohandas K. Gandhi

ON A VISIT TO ALBUQUERQUE, my life partner and I find a well-known organic and natural food store. I'm hoping to buy lavender flowers, so I can make my own sleeping potion. After years in the city, I still have trouble sleeping with cars going by twenty feet from my ears.

One of the joys of shopping in this particular store is the people who work here, people of every age, color, shape, size, and hairstyle, and all smiling. Apparently the store's policies don't require uniforms; I've seen employees wearing every conceivable mode of clothing, including flowing robes. We enjoy the refreshing contrast to the cowboy conservative look we grew up with; in our town, the western look is giving way to teenage girls in pajamas and teenage boys wearing pants falling off their hips and dragging the ground. Watching a couple of these victims of fashion try to run across the street can keep me giggling for blocks.

I first search unsuccessfully for lavender flowers in the herbal blossom section, then move in ever-increasing concentric circles out through other herbal beauty and health preparations. The degree of optimism or fantasy involved in either buying or selling some of these products ought to give us hope in a skeptical age, but I'm too cynical to buy most of the stuff.

By the time I realize I haven't found the lavender flowers, I've reached the meat counter and made smiling eye contact with a skinny guy wearing a cap the size of a prize-winning pumpkin. The cap is huge to accommodate a head full of springy, curly, bouncy hair. The words to the song from the musical *Hair* start tripping through my head: *Shining, gleaming, streaming, flaxen waxen.* His sidelocks dangle to his shoulders like the ringlets worn by Orthodox Jewish men. When I laugh with delight, he apparently reads my expression correctly, because his face lights up. I expect him to chime in with the words in my mind, *There ain't no words/ For the beauty, the splendor, the wonder of my hair.* But what he really says is, "May I help you?"

"I know it's not your department," I say, "but I can't find any lavender flowers with the other herbals."

"I'll get you the guy in charge of the lavender flower department," he replies, reaching for the phone. "He'll meet you back in that aisle."

"There's a department?" I mumble, but he's turned away.

I amble back to the aisle and find it fully occupied by a scrawny little Hispanic guy wearing earphones. He spins and twirls and snaps his fingers, bopping back and forth from the jars of herbal flowers on one side to the tofu scrub on the other. His wide pants drag on the floor, and with every other shimmy, he grabs one side or the other and yanks them up over his purple shorts. His shirt is unbuttoned, and his faux gold chains clank in time with some beat I can't hear. But I can almost see the beat: *snap, snatch, dip, sli-i-i-iiiide, snap, grab, bounce.*

I'll admit that I do not always feel warm around some of the gentlemen who dress in this manner because I've seen them selling drugs and waving knives and heard them make remarks in Spanish that I understand but would rather not translate for a family audience.

But this lad is a spinning top, a dervish of joy. He stands only a little higher than my belt buckle, and he is so happy that I can't help but smile.

He looks at me, and I see myself in his shades. Uh-oh. The white-haired gringo female is wearing a foolish smile, an ankle-length dress, and yellow rubber shoes. She looks like trouble. She makes eye contact.

I look around for the Lavender Flower Manager.

The Hispanic guy bobs up and down in front of me. "May I help you?" he says, rhythmically, and gestures at the shelves beside us. "This is my section."

Be-boppa, slide, shimmy, YANK.

"Ah—er—I'm looking for lavender flowers, and they don't seem to be here."

"I see that," he says. "Let me do some checking." Still bopping, he gyrates to the phone in the next aisle. I wander past some lipsticks and cosmetic creams, peering over the top of a display to see him talking on the phone, twisting and wriggling around the column holding the phone. I drift off, but I hear him hang up and dial again.

A few minutes later, I turn a corner and find him coming toward me. "Ma'am," he says, and then explains politely that the store's warehouse in Los Angeles does not have any lavender flowers. No other health food store in Albuquerque has lavender flowers. "There's a shortage," he says, "Worldwide; nobody has any lavender flowers. I am sorry."

I thank him for trying, for going to all the extra work of making additional calls. I smile. He smiles back. We stand, looking each other in the eye, for a long moment.

And then he bows and puts out his hand. I nod and bow my head and shake it, and he breaks into a huge grin and so do I and both of us shake hands a little longer, nodding and smiling at each other. Another few seconds of that and we'd have been dancing. We are both so happy to be friendly to one another.

And then I go on down the aisle toward Jerry, and the manager of the lavender flower division goes the other way. Each of us moves to our own music. But we look over our shoulders at each other, smiling. And we will both remember.

WARRIOR'S PENTACLE

Juniper Lauren

IN JULY 2013, SUZANNE EXTENDED AN INVITATION for the Living River, a group of pagan political activists, to join her under the dark moon and walk the Pentacle of the Warrior under the Texas capitol rotunda. Tejas witches have walked that pentacle for a couple of decades, tracing the star's five points inlaid within the marble floor, vocalizing a quiet tone beneath the granite dome, as Texas Rangers watch us from under the brims of their white cowboy hats and evaluate the terror potential of our meditation.

But this July was different. Wendy Davis, iconic in her sophisticated white suit and well-worn pink tennis shoes, had delayed the vote on a bill that would end safe abortion access for many Texas women. The tactics of the anti-abortion bill's supporters had defeated Wendy's filibuster, but in the last few moments before the constitutionally mandated end of the legislative session, thousands of Wendy supporters ran out the clock with a deafening roar, preventing a Senate vote. So Governor Perry had called the legislators back to Austin for a controversial special session to pass the bill.

Tonight the rotunda, usually almost empty but for the Rangers, was a swirling sea of bill proponents and opponents, flowing around families or couples there to sightsee. As I contemplated walking the pentacle, surrounded by blue-clad anti-abortion activists, I felt an unwarrior-like fear. Suzanne lead others along a path from point to point of the thirty-foot pentacle, while I studied the faces of those not walking, some in orange, some in blue, a few in the unaffiliated clothing of tourists. Eight teenagers in blue stood at one edge of the circle around the points, with red tape marking the word *LIFE* across their chests, singing all of the verses of "Amazing Grace" in angelic four-part harmony.

After watching a few moments, I walked to the north point, and stepped onto the pentacle path. Zee Helene was just ahead of me, her long, thick hair flowing and an orange belly dancer's scarf tied about her round, supple hips. Two young, dark-eyed girls stood with their mothers and brother on the edge of the circle surrounding the points. As Zee walked past the girls, they followed her onto our path, drawn by her pied-piper beauty.

As I approached their mothers, they stopped me with a smile and a question: "What are you doing?"

"We are walking a prayer to awaken the energies of the Warrior. Each point stands for one of the warrior powers: Commitment, Honor, Truth." I gestured toward one of the points with each word.

I had remembered the name for all of the points while walking, but in that moment I couldn't recall the point we were standing on. As Lisa made the turn, I asked her, "What is this point?"

"Strength."

"And Compassion," I said, gesturing toward the fifth point.

With their questions answered, I resumed my pentacle walk. Each time I approached the point where they continued to stand, one of the mothers, her dark eyes bright, softly spoke the word to remind me: "Strength."

ROSARY BEADS

Mary De Vries

MY MOTHER PULLED ME OUT OF PUBLIC SCHOOLS, but not because of any real principle along religious or moral lines. I could read at third grade level entering kindergarten, due to a bout of polio, and the public school wanted to place me in that grade. Mom said no and called her childhood pal, Father Kazmareck, and asked to enroll me at St. Teresa's, which was across the street from our house. So my life was set for several years. During the school week I did everything my classmates did: catechism, mass, daily Stations of the Cross during Lent, and all the prayers, including a daily rosary after lunch. Saturdays I attended the religious instruction at our Lutheran church.

Father Kaz highlighted most of my tenure at St. T's. He laughed, giggled, and slapped my mother's butt to get her attention when she was pulling weeds. Why did he do it? To make sure that she, and only she, would pack his lunch for the school picnic. He was a Hawaiian-shirted, khaki-pants priest who made life and religion joyful, if not very serious. However, all that was to change when his assistant pastor arrived in my sixth-grade year.

Father Ritz was an escapee from behind the Curtain, where practicing any religious faith could mean death. Perhaps that, though we students did not think of it at the time, explained the man, who was a polar opposite to Kaz. Father Ritz—to this day I cannot shorten his title—wore cassocks so starched that the edges looked like knives, and only during mass was the biretta gone from his head. He walked so quietly that he was behind you before you knew it. If you were "sinning," his hand would go to your shoulder and he would march you to the chapel, where you and he would sit in silent contemplation of your error. Not one word of displeasure or reprimand, just silence until the words "forgive me" issued forth from your lips and several Hail Marys were assigned. That silence was more forceful than all the laughing *do not do it again* from Kaz.

Friday confessions were fraught with wonderment and fear. Who was the priest in the booth? As a Protestant, I sat closest to the booth in the Mary row (yes, we had ten Marys in my class and we had our own pew). The Marys expected me to check out the shoes beneath the curtain. Loafers or sandals peeking beneath the scarlet drape, and they breathed a sigh of relief. If the shoes shone like patent leather and were laced oxfords, they began to reduce the things they would confess.

Ritz was not feared, but he was not attainable. Silence surrounded him. Idle conversation was not his style. When he spoke, it mattered. The only time I feared him was the day I asked if Mary had other children after Jesus. His hand slowly rose, with a finger pointing to the door, as he quietly said, "Out, Protestant." Yet, to give him his due, he was also the one whose hand on my shoulder brought me back into class, as he whispered a quiet "Forgive me." An adult who could admit his error—I was stunned.

Yet the image that still moves me is another one of near silence. Having forgotten my school bag in the chapel, I ran across the street after supper to retrieve it. Going down the chapel stairs, I stopped when I noticed someone praying. Father Ritz knelt in a pew, evening sunlight streaming on him from the stained glass window. His hands—so long, lean and strong—were moving his wooden rosary beads as tears flowed down his cheeks. I stood for a moment in a silence broken only by the clacking beads and then I tiptoed up the stairs. My schoolbag could wait; I was sure I had seen a saint.

HEART

Jeanne Guy

MY HUSBAND'S FATHER DIED ON CHRISTMAS EVE 2011 from a rapid onset of acute myeloid leukemia, so our holidays were bittersweet. While it was fast, with little pain, and Hospice Odyssey helped us all as we sat vigil from the date of diagnosis (December 17) until he died, it was just such a shock. We picture him now dancing with his wife, who died a mere eleven months earlier. What a wonderful New Year's Eve they will have.

The following is what I wrote on Tuesday morning, December 20, 2011, while still at the hospital with him:

They've taken him away. He was sleeping as I held his hand, kissed his forehead and said I love you, before the attendant rolled the hospital bed out into the long hall, heading to wherever procedures are done.

We have all been reassured that the bone marrow biopsy my father-in-law is about to have is much improved since the days my sister-in-law had hers, 26 years previously. She had Hodgkin's lymphoma, and thanks to early detection and treatment, received a clean bill of health and is with us today.

My 85-year-old father-in-law apparently doesn't have the urinary tract infection first suspected when the family brought him, weak and tired, to the ER three days ago. According to initial tests, we're looking at a leukemia diagnosis; the bone marrow biopsy will let us know.

This funny curmudgeon of a man lost his partner of 62 years to Alzheimer's less than a year ago. Though he is in a lovely retirement center, her loss left a hole in his heart that even the nicest of facilities could not comfort. Lacking caregiving skills, he was at a loss even before she died, as he watched her fade. He was famous for saying "we're fine" when neither he nor she was even close to being okay. He wanted so badly for her to get better.

This morning, while Dad was gone for the procedure, a hospital volunteer came by. This attractive retired woman had stopped by unannounced with a newspaper for me. "You have a little glitter on your face," she said and gently removed it. I laughed as I explained it must have come from the sparkly Christmas boxes sitting next to my makeup mirror. I thanked her and said, "I don't know. Maybe we all could use more glitter about now," and started to tear up unexpectedly. "It doesn't look good for him, my father-in-law." She stayed with me a while and listened while I spoke of both the leukemia and the metaphorical hole in his heart.

After Dad was brought back to the room, Kay, the kind volunteer, stopped by to check on us and said, "I have a present for you." She gave me a wrapped, heart-shaped ornament, the size and thickness of the palm of my hand. It smelled wonderful, filled with a deep woods fresh pine scent, like my house at Christmas time when I was a child.

Dad is still sleeping and I am writing, and praying inadequate prayers. Comfort and joy. I pray for comfort and joy for him and his family.

I hold my new ornament in my lap as I type, and the scented gift fills my head with memories of my mother and those long-ago Christmases. Kay the volunteer is now gone; I remove the sparkly, wide red ribbon on the package and unwrap it to get a better look at my unexpected treasure.

Glitter. Silver glitter covers the entire heart.

She brought me a glittered heart. I cry.

I reach for Dad's hand and place this new treasure in it. He continues to sleep as he has for the last three days but his big hand tightens around the comfort and joy that an angel named Kay brought us.

I'm thinking it would be a good idea for all of us to glitter our hearts and share them over the holidays and in the days ahead. If you do, I bet you'll experience that same comfort and joy. After all, we could all use a little glitter right now.

THE CAT CAME BACK

Jude Walsh

WE WERE A DOG FAMILY. I can mark time by which dog we had when. As a toddler, I remember Blackie, the cocker spaniel who would eat a bit of aspirin ground up in some jelly so I would have the courage to do the same. There was Clancy, a border collie mix that tolerated being dressed in my dresses and hats and being squeezed into a doll carriage as my baby. Patricia, the Irish setter, was a short-timer. We had to give her to a friend who lived way out in the country with no near neighbors because she would not stop stealing laundry from our neighbors' clotheslines. When I was in junior high, we had Pedro, a miniature rat terrier whose most distinguishing characteristic was his shivering. And finally, there was Henry, an English springer spaniel. My mother and I had food poisoning when Henry arrived; we were quite ill. Despite our suffering, my dad brought the puppy to us and said we could name her. In our delirium, we missed the "her" part and tossed out Henry. When we were well enough to cuddle the puppy, we realized our mistake. My father thought the whole thing made a great story so her name stuck, despite Mom's suggestion to change it to Henrietta.

We never had cats. My father didn't like them and my mother still harbored some old-wives'-tale fear about cats stealing a sleeping baby's breath. We were long past the baby stage in our house when my older sister brought home Pierre. Pierre was a gray and white boy with a devil-may-care attitude and a desire to be outdoors more than in. My sister begged and pleaded and generally wore my parents down. I didn't care one way or the other, staying centered in the we-are-dog-people belief.

Soon after, my sister went off to nursing school, leaving Pierre in our care. And darned if we didn't develop a fondness for the critter. If we wanted to call the cat home, one of us would shake a box of Friskies, a dry cat food popular at the time. Pierre would appear, and come into the house for his bowl of food and a good night's sleep.

One fall day, Pierre did not come when I shook the box. I was not overly concerned, thinking he had wandered out of hearing range. I tried again later that night, still no Pierre. It would not be the first time he had spent a night outdoors. When he had done so before, he was always meowing at the back door in the morning, demanding breakfast since he'd missed his dinner. But not this time. First days, then weeks went by without Pierre's return. My stoic father made scathing remarks like, "You can't trust a cat. The *omadhaun** probably got himself killed in a fight or hit by a car." I wasn't sure what either of those things had to do with trust, but I knew it was my dad's way of admitting he missed the cat.

That January, during a snowstorm, about nine o'clock at night, my family was gathered around the kitchen table having what we referred to as a "snack." What that meant was my mother, father, grandmother, and aunt were all at the table having sandwiches made from fresh cold cuts on thick slices of bread with cheese and mayonnaise or mustard, with sides of potato chips and dill pickles. They were having an ice-cold beer or two to wash it down. I was there as well but my beverage was a mug of piping hot, strong black tea with cream and sugar. My dad was, as usual, entertaining us with stories from his youth and from working in the mines. It was a wicked night, the wind howling and forcing cold air through the sash windows, sleety snow striking the panes. We were warm and cozy and enjoying one another's company when I thought I heard something. I asked them all to be quiet. A ridiculous request to an Irish family in the midst of beer and storytelling, but finally I persuaded them.

"Listen! I think I hear something." They got quiet for a minute but nothing aside from the storm was heard.

"No, no," I insisted, "I thought I heard a meow." I opened the back door, ushering in a gust of wind and cold. Grabbing the box of Friskies still sitting by the door, I gave it a good long shake and yelled, "Pierre!" My family was howling in protest. "Shut the door! You'll freeze us all! That cat is long gone!"

I gave the box one more good shake and was turning to come in when something brushed against my legs. It was Pierre, scrambling in like he never had before. He was caked in sleet and his tail was broken, bent at an unnatural angle, the end appearing completely frozen.

Well, there was much rejoicing at the table. We all took a turn holding the cat and rubbing him briskly, trying to get the icy chunks out of his fur. He was less than pleased with our ministrations. Once we put him down, he went straight to where his bowl used to be and waited. I got out a bowl, filled it with Friskies and supplied water as well. While he crunched away, I got him a new cushion and warmed a towel for him to rest on as he continued to thaw.

The next morning, he was warm and dry and right back on his old schedule of spending the day outdoors and being called home by the rattling of the Friskies box each night. We never knew where he had been or why he decided to return. We just accepted it: the cat came back.

Omadhaun: a Gaelic word meaning "a fool." Used in ethnic Irish neighborhoods to describe a stupid or dumb person.

CULINARY TREASURES

Sara Etgen-Baker

MOTHER'S RECTANGULAR KITCHEN WAS TINY—no more than seven feet long and five feet wide—which was to be expected since the house itself was small. When my parents moved into their two-bedroom house in 1952, the kitchen—designed primarily for functionality—came equipped with a moderate-sized refrigerator and a full-size gas range, but little storage space. Storage was so scarce that mother kept her pots and pans in the oven overnight and removed them the next morning when she prepared breakfast.

I learned to cook standing alongside her but often complained about her cramped, cracker-box kitchen. "I hate cooking in here! It's hot and there's no room to breathe." I'd open the kitchen window and fan myself rather dramatically. "You know, clean up would be easier if you just had a dishwasher and disposal."

"When I was a young girl during the Depression, I helped my mother cook on a wood stove that was so old it had holes in it." Mother stopped what she was doing and grabbed her wet dishtowel. "Look around. My kitchen has a stove, a refrigerator, pots, pans, and cooking utensils; everything else is optional." Then she whipped her dishtowel between her thumbs and forefingers and snapped it on my buttocks. "Don't be so fussy!"

After dinner, I usually hand-washed and dried the dishes, while my mother, aunt, and grandmother huddled around Mother's tiny kitchen table. They dumped all their S&H Green Stamps onto the table, sorted them by denomination, licked them, and then stuck them on the grid pages of the booklets that the supermarket gave away.

Like most women in the 1950s and early 1960s, Mother didn't work outside the home and didn't have an income of her own. Collecting and redeeming Green Stamps gave her a feeling of independence and a means of obtaining items she wanted or needed. Occasionally, my grandmother gave my mother filled stamp books so Mother could purchase what she needed. Even with my grandmother's help, Mother saved for two years before she had enough stamps for an electric waffle-maker and mixer.

The day Mother redeemed her stamps, I went with her to the Redemption Center. "Here." She handed me a blank order form. "I forgot my glasses and need you to fill this in for me." While we waited for the stockroom clerk to check their inventory, I browsed through the store.

Then I saw it—*The Betty Crocker Cookbook for Boys and Girls*—aptly described as a great cookbook for children, introducing them to basic cooking techniques and easy recipes. I slid my fingers across the pages and glanced through the recipes, drawings and photographs, and knew that I simply must have that cookbook. Although the cookbook cost only half a book of Green Stamps, I knew better than to out-and-out ask Mother to give me any of her precious Green Stamps! So I formulated a foolproof plan.

"Mother." I paused at the cookbook display. "Have you seen this cookbook?" I opened the book's pages. "It's just perfect for me, and . . ."

"Hmm." Mother turned a few pages. "I don't know. Half a book of stamps is . . ."

"I know, but I'll do extra chores to earn enough stamps to buy it. Please, Mother, *pleeeese!*"

"I s'pose so. But you're responsible for your own stamps and putting them in the booklet." She returned the book to the display. "And once school starts, you won't be able to do as many extra chores. School comes first."

Determined, I spent the entire summer doing extra chores—ironing my father's shirts, folding clothes, vacuuming, and dusting. At some point, even the neighbor ladies helped; they gave me Green Stamps for polishing their shoes, ironing their clothes, washing their dishes, dusting their houses, and running errands to the nearby supermarket. I was so ecstatic that I even stopped complaining about Mother's kitchen. But by summer's end, I was two pages short of having the half-book of Green Stamps that I needed.

Once school started, I did as I promised and dedicated myself to my schoolwork. The fall and winter months passed, and by Christmas I still didn't have enough stamps to buy my cookbook. Then one December evening while sipping on his coffee, my father asked, "Sweetie Pie, how many more stamps do you need for your cookbook?"

"Just two more pages, Daddy. Why? Do you have an errand or chore for me?"

"Yes, I do." He placed his cup on the table. "Tell you what—grab your coat and stamps and hop in my pickup."

I followed him to the truck, hoisted myself onto the seat, and noticed an envelope with my name on it.

"What's this, Daddy?"

"Go ahead, open it."

When I did, loose green stamps poured out onto the seat. "Are all these for me?"

"Yes, Sweetie Pie!"

"But how, Daddy?"

"A few months ago, my gas station started giving Green Stamps, so I've saved these for you as part of your Christmas present. Merry Christmas!" I squealed and hugged him. "Now let's go get that cookbook!"

He immediately drove to the Redemption Center where I filled in the order form and received my cookbook. At home, father inscribed these words on the inside cover: *May this, your first cookbook, help you to learn to love cooking. Love, Daddy, Christmas 1961.*

"Pick a recipe, Daddy, and I'll make it for you."

He flipped through the pages. "How 'bout this Eskimo Igloo Cake?"

So on that Christmas and many Christmases thereafter, I made the Eskimo Igloo Cake just for Father—our very own father-daughter tradition. Now—more than fifty years later—I miss baking my father's special cake in my mother's cracker-box kitchen. I miss sitting at Mother's kitchen table and licking green stamps; and I miss cooking in close proximity to my mother. Sometimes, though, as I putter around my spacious kitchen, I feel my parents' presence and treasure the culinary moments we shared.

NOT ENOUGH

Mignon Martin

MY PARENTS SHARED A GREAT ROMANCE, but it pales in intensity when compared to the romance I had with my mother. Although I was only one of her seven children, I knew early that ours was a powerful passion, which was essential to my sanity.

I sat in her lap and traced the veins in her hands with my little fingers, and when she took a nap, I sulked until she reappeared. I accompanied her everywhere, listening to her voice, savoring her manner with the boy who carried her groceries, the lady at the bank, and Evelyn, her hairdresser. She was utterly charming. Warm and witty. A grand and southern lady.

She was always interested—interested in my latest drawing, the spot on my dress, and the hurt in my heart. She held me and kissed me and told me she loved me. She told me I could do anything and be anybody. She showed me how to mix a cake and how to argue. She gave me spankings and huge birthday parties. She prayed for me and made me take piano lessons far past the time I begged to quit. I supposed each of my siblings had equally intense relationships with my mother, but I didn't care. Clearly, she could demand anyone's heart, so I simply celebrated that she seemed to want mine. She was, and she filled me up, and that was enough.

On the night of their twelfth wedding anniversary, I was sullen and brooding as I pondered the evening without her in it. I lay across her bed, flipping through *Aesop's Fables*, waiting for her to dress. When she stepped out of the closet, I caught my breath. She wore pink linen with pearls and sequins sprinkled across the bodice. Just below her slim hips, the hem flared, stopping right above her perfect knees. Her neck was circled by tiny pink pearls, her ears shimmered with matching clips, and little pink bows hovered on the toes of her shoes. She crossed the room to sit at her dressing table and began to pile her long, dark hair high on her head. She opened a drawer and took out a pair of pink combs made of pearls and sequins and delicate, pink, spun-sugar feathers. She carefully placed one behind each ear and turned for my opinion.

At six years old, sprawled across my mother's bed, I knew beautiful for the first time.

I couldn't breathe, and I wanted to cry, and I needed words I didn't have.

The Alzheimer's unit is called "The Courtyards." There aren't any—courtyards, I mean—because they have to keep all the doors locked to prevent residents from wandering out onto the Interstate. Just a couple of sad wrought iron tables sit beside a fishless pond in an inaccessible outside area. I visit when I'm in town, and when I can stand it.

I follow her from the dining room to the TV room, trying to hide my face. I take her arm and don't want to let go. I fix her hair and kiss her and tell her I love her. She sits in a rocking chair wearing a pink duster, her legs daintily crossed at her ankles, smiling a blank sweetness. My flight leaves in an hour, so I put my head in her lap before I go.

I can't breathe, and I want to cry, and I need words I don't have.

INVISIBLE

Lucy Painter

Tap, tap. I felt a small pat on my arm as I picked out oranges from a pyramid at Sweet Bay Grocery on Beneva Road. My mind was five blocks away, back at the animal shelter, where I had spent the afternoon trying to teach Big Otis to walk calmly on his leash, not successfully. Today the goofy hound had won our battle of wills. I was sweaty, hot, tired, decidedly dirty, and looking forward to home and a cool shower.

Tap, tap. Irritated, I turned my head to locate the interruption.

Nothing. There was no one there. At least, that is what I thought until I looked down. Next to me, and reaching not quite to my shoulder, stood a tiny old woman, her arthritic hand on my sweaty arm.

"Dearie." She looked up at me with faded blue eyes. "Can you give me a ride home? I walked here but am too tired to walk back." The accent was something foreign, maybe Eastern European. She looked very old, her face a map of wrinkles and lines etched into leathery skin. Her shiny black suit, once elegant and expensive, hung on her frame but lent her an air of Old World dignity. Around her neck draped a bright red and purple scarf, damp now with her sweat.

"Of course we can," Charlie, my husband, answered from behind me. "Where do you live?"

She gave us the address, one I recognized as in a neighborhood not far away along busy Fruitville Road, an obstacle course for even the young spry pedestrian, much less an elderly little woman.

Holding tightly to my arm, she crossed the parking lot with us in slow measured steps and allowed Charlie to lift her into the rear seat of our SUV, packed with dog leashes and dirty T-shirts from our day at the shelter. Ignoring the mess, she daintily pulled her skirt over her skinny knees and sat upright, her tiny feet dangling from the high seat. She reminded me of our children, of the expression on their faces as we set out for ice cream or a trip to the park, expectant and happy.

As Charlie maneuvered through the heavy traffic on Fruitville Road, she told us her story. Her voice carried softly from the back seat.

"My husband and I came here many years ago. We were so happy then, had so much to look forward to. We knew all of our neighbors and all of their children, who used to play in each other's yards and ride bicycles to school together and fish in the canal over there." She pointed to a slim thread of water in the distance.

"But that was then," she continued. "Our children are gone now, moved away. They say they are too busy to come to Florida to see me. Our son, Detrick, has a big job up in New York, but he always sends a Christmas card. And they all came down to their father's funeral last year. Last September it was, almost a year ago now."

No one spoke as we turned onto her street, a short dead-end road of the small bungalows so popular in 1950s Florida. The sidewalks remained, but the trees had been cut down, leaving the little houses to bake in the sun, the surrounding grass burned to dust. Broken toys, plastic and faded, littered the yards, and white Styrofoam cups gathered at the edge of drainage culverts. Next to broken porches sat old trucks, some without tires, propped up on blocks and dripping oil onto the dirt. In grimy windows hung aluminum blinds at crazy angles. Not a human face appeared, only the tinny sound of a cheap radio blasting percussion into the hot still air. The street was empty, except for a black dog skulking along a fence. With a low growl, he turned to glance at us before darting into an alley.

"That's my house, number 14," she whispered from the back seat as Charlie slowed to avoid a black trash bag lying in the street. Her lawn, surrounded by a chain link fence, needed mowing, and weeds poked their heads through the lattice. But her shades were evenly pulled and her front porch swept clean. Pots of red geraniums flanked the white front door, and in the front window sat a large yellow cat, perking its ears as we approached.

Looking warily at the little house, Charlie asked, "Are you okay here? By yourself?"

"Yes, I think so," she sighed. "I don't know my neighbors now, don't know who they are or what they do. They don't speak to me, but they leave me alone. Their children play in the street, but they don't come into my yard, so I don't even know their names. But I'm all right here. It's OK."

Charlie lifted her down and helped her through the gate, while the cat stretched and yawned in the window. We watched her unlock the front door and enter the little house, alone and invisible.

NURTURING

Essays from
Real Women Write

2015

WARRIOR MOTHER

Lois Ann Bull

IN 1941, ARMED ONLY WITH BANANAS, my mother tried to control her world. Bombs burst, guns flared, people died in Europe and the Pacific while Mom battled on the home front.

My brother, Ron, was very ill. When he was fourteen months old, she mentioned concerns to the family GP. He passed off the lack of weight gain to "He's a late bloomer," and the same for not having the strength to walk. When she sought another opinion, the next doctor accused her of imagining problems and inventing illnesses. Intuitively, this valedictorian of both her high school and college knew better. The British Lion inside her fought on, seeking answers.

When the child lost his attention span and could no longer hold his head up, she began calling hospital personnel, begging for referrals. Finally, a name in Newark, New Jersey, surfaced: Dr. Philip Graham, a pediatrician (a new term for Mom who didn't know that some doctors specialized in children's medicine). He saw them the next day.

Dr. Graham listened to my mom's observations and then examined the skinny little boy. Finally, he said gently, "Your son is starving to death. That's why he's so quiet. Your instincts are right. He's very sick."

She sat motionless, a corner of her lower lip tensely caught between her teeth. Barely breathing, she prayed he knew what to do.

"Your baby's not getting any nutrition from his food because he can't absorb it. I think it may be celiac disease. He can't digest gluten."

"How did he get this disease?" Mom asked.

"We think some children are born with it."

"What's going to happen to my little boy?"

"There is no known cure, no medicine. All we can do is try to prevent him from dying of malnutrition. If we can get him strong, maybe he'll be able to tolerate some foods. Start with a diet of bananas. They digest easily. It will help his intestines heal and mature."

"What other foods can he have?" Mom asked.

"No other food. Twenty a day. Ripe. If you can't get bananas, then buy banana flakes at the druggist. Be patient. It could take several years before he's better."

The length of time for recovery didn't alarm my mother. Now she knew what plagued her son; she had a diagnosis and treatment plan; her enemy had a face and she could do battle. Now that she was in charge, the word *impossible* didn't exist.

On the way home, she stopped at the grocer. She would buy all the bananas. It never occurred to her they might not have any. Therefore, when she couldn't find any, she asked the manager, "What time tomorrow will you have bananas?"

"I'm sorry, Madam, but I don't know when in the near future we'll see bananas."

"But you always have bananas." Her voice rose.

"Lady," he retorted, "There's a war on. There aren't any ships. The government took them all for troops." He threw up his hands in defeat.

Mom had been so concerned about Ron's condition that she'd forgotten about war and shortages. Not wanting to use precious gasoline, she went home and called other food stores looking for bananas. No luck. Desperate, determined, and having nowhere else to turn, she called the police. Did they know where she could get a prolonged supply of bananas for her sick child who would otherwise die?

The police called back. Mr. Ceircy in Paterson, New Jersey, a fruit wholesaler for the United Shipping Lines, still could get bananas. Telephoning him, my mother explained what she needed and why. Her persuasive speech touched Mr. Ceircy's heart. He promised to supply her with all she needed.

We'd arrive for our pick-up and go to the front of the line with our doctor's prescription. With few words, more like grunts, this stocky, stoop-shouldered, white-haired man in a green apron brusquely loaded a complete branch into the trunk of our car. Week after week, he always saved enough for Ron and, in so doing, saved his life.

Throughout the war, our house resembled a tropical jungle. Big stalks, with multiple hands of green fruit, rested in our cool basement, waiting their turn to keep Ron alive. Dad would lift the 65- to 100-pound stalk out of the car when he arrived home from work and carry it down the stairs. Every morning, Mom hacked off a tier of twenty or so and brought them upstairs to exchange for ripe ones on our windowsills and tables—the day's ration. Green, yellow, and gold dotted the household. She'd slice, dice, mash, smash, whole, halve, or quarter them.

If Dad traveled on one of his frequent auditing trips, Mom would slash hands of bananas off while the stalk still sat in the car trunk. Ron and I stood clear while she wielded the carving knife like a battle-axe. Then she'd carry them to the basement.

Once she had used most of the bananas, those left would suddenly ripen faster than my brother could eat them. Neighbors happily bought them.

By year's end, Ron's alertness had returned, his cheeks rounded, and he had begun to walk. With the improvements, Dr. Graham permitted the introduction of a few new foods very slowly—first baked potatoes, then lean meat, then butter came next, along with buttermilk and still more bananas. The meat and butter were rationed, as was the gas. Even worse, sometimes grocers would only permit one stick of butter or one pound of meat for each five dollars spent. Mom would go all over town to do her shopping piecemeal, using up valuable time and gas. Fortunately, family and friends shared their own rations to be sure Ron got enough to eat.

My mother fought for six years, conquering each obstacle as it arose. I was two months old when her battle started. My memories begin about age three. The ordeal consumed the whole family, and I absorbed her fighting spirit and unwillingness to give up.

Ron lived. He is now seventy-six years old.

FRAGMENTS FROM MY CHILDHOOD

Sipra Roy

I GREW UP IN 1940s INDIA with parents, grandparents, siblings, and cousins. My mother was kind and soft-spoken. My father was a loving patriarch whom we adored. He worked for the Indian Railways and we moved often. As India celebrated independence from centuries of British rule, we moved to a quaint town named Madhupur. It had been built to remind former residents of the English villages they left and missed—mansions, manicured lawns, churches. Railway employees were now housed in those mansions.

Outside, the atmosphere at home was very festive. But I was not as cheerful as I should have been, growing up in that loving environment. I carried a sense of melancholy, sometimes for reasons unknown, throughout my life.

My father was the third of six brothers. His eldest brother was an eccentric popular scholar and a professor at a prestigious university in another city. My father took up the responsibility of his brother's four children, to allow his brother to continue his scholarly pursuits undisturbed. His brother seemed to enjoy this arrangement.

His eldest daughter, Renuka, who stayed with us, was beautiful. She was my mother's confidante in managing our large family. Word of her beauty spread, and brought many marriage proposals. My uncle relieved himself of the responsibility of Renuka's marriage and was happy for my father to make the decisions. Arranged marriages were the norm and were considered the parents' responsibility—a daughter's marriage was a great burden given the social pressure to get them married young and the financial pressure of sending the daughter to her in-laws' home with jewelry and gifts. Marriage negotiations involved a complex routine of exploring families, the bride's homemaking skills and beauty, and the groom's job prospects. Finally, a groom was chosen for Renuka.

My father wanted to celebrate this marriage magnificently to keep up the family status. He distributed the expenditure among his five brothers according to their financial capacity, while he took up the largest share. Renuka's father was tasked to buy gold jewelry for the bride and groom.

The week of the marriage, a massive gazebo was set up. An Indian flute played in the background while all the children played under the gazebo. My uncles gave my father their parts of the expense. Except for Renuka's father. Then, on the day before the wedding, I witnessed a drama unnoticed by most.

My mother insisted that Renuka's father show the jewelry he was responsible for. He sat calmly with eyes closed. My father stood at the door of the room. On being pressed more, her father said, "Renuka is beautiful, many princes will come for her hand even without jewelry; let us break this alliance." First there was silence, then disbelief, and then my father was furious at his brother's suggestion and the thought of what this meant. At one point, my frustrated father said, "Bring me a gun, I will kill him and me."

My mother somehow managed to pacify the warring brothers. All the thrill of a wedding vanished like camphor for me. Like a shadow, I followed my mother, who slipped into the dimly lit room where Renuka was sitting with her mother.

Mother told Renuka that her father wanted the marriage to be called off. Renuka embraced my mother and began to cry inconsolably, "Please do not listen to that crazy man. I will marry here, otherwise I will kill myself!"

My mother said, "But Renu, we do not have money to purchase the jewelry needed to marry you." Then, she went on, "Since we cannot marry you without jewelry, maybe I will loan you my wedding jewelry. Let's keep it a secret, okay? But promise me that you will return it all to me, because this is all I have to give for my daughter's wedding."

Renuka and her mother leaped at the proposal. "Let us get the marriage ceremony done peacefully and we will return it. We are ever grateful to you."

My mother left, and in the dark of that room, I saw the faces of Renuka and her mother awash with a satisfied glow. In the evening, all the women sat around the bride and praised the jewelry and how she looked like a princess. My mother sat next to her with pride, partly at averting a family disaster and partly at the appreciation of her jewelry. I sat there blankly and listened to the nostalgic tunes of the Indian flute, which stirred a strong ennui in me about days gone by and what lay ahead, the happiness all around but the sad undertones of this festivity, which I had witnessed.

I wore a brocade dress but the drama of the morning had drained me; before I knew it, I was asleep. I woke up late in the night and ran across the courtyard to the gazebo. Renuka and the groom stood by the fire, as the priest chanted wedding vows. The courtyard was lit with lanterns and my sister and her husband looked angelic. I was hungry but could not find any food. Tired, I fell asleep again in the dimly lit room where so much drama had unfolded earlier in the day.

Soon after, my own sister, Mira, was married in another wonderful ceremony, leaving my father submerged in debt from frequent marriage and medical expenses. Every year, Renuka and her husband visited us—she never mentioned the wedding jewelry or returned it. Neither did my mother mention the loan or ask her for it. I never heard my parents regret or boast of this act of sacrifice, even in the worst of their financial struggles. Much to my surprise, my mother seemed glad about Renuka's happy married life and spoke of her with great affection.

So often in life, underneath the joy and festivity lies the reality of a less joyous story. My heart fills with pride thinking about the nobility of my father and gentle mother and how they went about it all so gracefully.

BREAD ON THE GRASS

Linda C. Wisniewski

"WE DON'T THROW AWAY BREAD," MY MOTHER SAID. She took a few quick steps to the metal trashcan near the kitchen sink and fished out the crusts inside.

It might have been a Saturday with both of us home at lunchtime. I would have been small, maybe seven. She probably made me a bologna sandwich with mayonnaise and a slice of tomato on Lady Betty bread and poured me a glass of milk. Lady Betty smiled at me from the outside of the white plastic bread bag, her hair in a curly brown up-do.

"Grandma says bread is like the Host," my mother said, holding my discarded crusts in her outstretched hand. She meant the communion wafer, transformed at Sunday Mass into the body of Christ.

Grandma was Mom's best friend and confidante, the one she turned to when life was hard and there were no easy answers. She had come to Amsterdam, New York, at the turn of the twentieth century, and now lived in a second floor flat, with no telephone or hot running water, seeing no need for either. During the Great Depression, each of her six children, one by one, left school as soon as they were old enough to look for work. Nobody wasted so much as a crust of bread.

An old Polish proverb says, "A guest in the home is God in the home." Most of Grandma's guests were family, but as soon as anyone crossed her doorstep, she scurried to the cupboard for cake, donuts, potato chips, any food she could offer. For this wife of a grocery clerk, store-bought food meant she had money.

She taught me to say *chleb*, the Polish word for bread, as she sliced a fresh loaf, giving it her full attention, making of the act a little ritual of gratitude. I never saw her toss away a single morsel.

As I chewed on my crust-less sandwich, my mother stood beside me wearing her homemade skirt and a white blouse. Beneath her curly brown hair, the look on her face was serious but kind.

"We can feed the birds," she said.

We tore the crusts into little pieces and piled them on my empty plate. I imagined tiny beaks happily munching, thanks to Mom, Lady Betty, and me. Mom turned the worn brass handle on the back porch door, pulled it open and solemnly handed me the plate. I carried it as reverently as I had seen the altar boys carry the golden paten of consecrated hosts on Sunday morning.

Then Mom and I threw handfuls of the torn bread out the porch window. I waited for little birds to fly into our yard and discover the feast, but none came. Quickly bored, I went back inside. The next morning, when I looked out the window, the bread was gone. Shy birds, I thought, like me, but at least they won't go hungry.

After I grew up and married, I learned to bake bread from a cookbook. All-natural was the way to go, in food as well as childbirth. There would be no store-bought bread in my home. That approach lasted a year or two, until I had a full time job and a long commute. Because it was so easy to buy a loaf at the supermarket, I declared bread-baking a skill for hippies and earth mothers who did not work outside the home. We met friends for dinner at restaurants, everyone too busy to cook.

At home, my little boys left their sandwich crusts on their plates, just as their mother did long ago. You can guess what I told them.

"We don't throw away bread," I said. "We can feed the birds."

I showed them how to tear the crusts into pieces and scatter them on the grass for our feathered guests. Sometimes they even stayed to watch the birds peck at it.

Now that our nest is empty, bread is a high carb item my husband and I have cut back on. We keep our whole-wheat loaf in the fridge, but it still goes stale. Nobody wants the ends, dented and misshapen in the plastic bag. Outside my window, five bird feeders hold sunflower seeds, split peanuts, and calcium-rich suet for strong eggshells. I have a discount club membership at the birdseed store. But none of that feels quite so holy as the simple act of tossing breadcrumbs on the grass.

CLOUD FORMATIONS

Lanie Tankard

THE CLOUD WAVED AT ME, skipping along outside my window that sunny morning. It was a low cumulus—a distinct little thermal puff resembling a cauliflower, bowled with great velocity high into the sky, ascending rapidly and riotously.

My breath caught in surprise. I wanted to stop it, hug it tight, halt its upward journey away from me as it romped toward the heavens. Surely I could do that. I had magical powers, didn't I? After all, I was a mother.

Oh, how I stretched, trying to reach high enough, hard enough, long enough, so I could grasp that spritely little whiff of white. Both arms—one still hooked up to the IV, I ignored the pain as I pulled against the tube implanted on the back of my wrist—reaching, reaching, reaching for that hazy flying mass of water particles as it cavorted ever upward.

Then the tiny cloud seemed to pause and turn. For the briefest moment, I had the uncanny sensation it was sending a wink and a smile my way, like a surrealist cloud painting by René Magritte with images from my unconscious mind creatively juxtaposed. Reality or illusion?

"Stop!" I cried.

"Wait," I pleaded.

"Don't go," I begged.

"Please come back," I whispered.

"Just for a minute," I sobbed.

My magical powers weren't working. The minuscule soul riding that gust of air like a raft in the sky was now out of sight. One particular possibility had simply vanished, a thought not yet formed. This potential for full creation at nine months had fallen far short at a mere eight weeks. How dare the sun shine today?!

The prospect of a spring baby to play with two eager sisters was over. *Fini.* That story line had just been deleted. More physical evidence of the love my husband and I had for one another was wiped out. I blew a kiss out the hospital window as bright light filled my eyes with tears. I left, bereft and bewildered.

The first two pregnancies had been easy, although one delivery barely escaped tragedy. Our second daughter was born five minutes after my arrival at that same hospital. The neonatologist said she wouldn't have survived without the expertise of my obstetrician.

But this—never had I imagined my third pregnancy could end at two months, nor that I would find it difficult to walk for several weeks after a D&C. Since I hadn't heard miscarriages talked about much at all, how could I have even considered the chance? Such resounding silence about an event so emotionally charged was simply unnerving. How common is it, I wondered? Naturally, we grieve later-term pregnancy losses and stillborn babies, but no rituals seem to exist to aid in mourning the evaporation of a little cloud.

Friends tried to cheer me up with comments like "You can have another," while my brain screamed, "But I can't have that one, conceived under a particular set of circumstances, imbued with the spirits of who we were that moment, due to be born at a certain season of the year." I averted my eyes when pregnant bellies loomed in my peripheral vision. I grieved mightily for the fragment of tissue that had left me. Tears bubbled up with no warning.

Once, as I sat in our living room, they began cascading over my cheeks. I bent double, placing my hands over my face. My youngest daughter watched for a moment, then dashed down the hall to her room. She returned in a flash. I felt something soft shoved up between my elbows. Peeking between my tears, I saw it was her DeeDee—a hemmed square of white fabric with blue polka dots, made by a friend when she was born. The cloth had become her comfort blankie, a talisman at times of trouble. And here she was, offering it up in two-year-old empathy, brow knitted and tongue clenched.

I took her on my lap, cuddling her with one arm and clasping DeeDee with the other to dab my eyes. I told her I was sad because the little baby growing inside me had been too weak to continue and because I knew she'd make a wonderful big sister—just like her own big sister (then six). She nodded, snuggling closer.

And sure enough, about ten months later next fall, I departed the same hospital once again, this time with my third daughter tucked safely in my arms. Joy reigned that day. I could never have imagined it a year earlier, when I watched that tiny little cloud drift away. Now my three girls are my best friends. I am full of love for those young women.

So, how can I explain this? Afterward, every five or ten years, for reasons I couldn't figure out, my heart would give a little lurch when I'd notice a random young boy at a park, in a crowd, on the street. What could have drawn my attention to this handful of growing men-in-the-making? Why did my breath catch when I saw one? I didn't know them. What I felt strongly each time was: I bet that's what my son would have been like.

Perhaps one never fully gets over a searing experience, but rather knits it into the fabric of life henceforward. By so doing, it's possible for clouds to continue to communicate with us, long after the breeze has blown them out of sight. Cloud formations indicate the type of weather ahead. Maybe that perky little cloud had been forecasting bliss on the horizon with my third daughter.

Today I have two fine sons-in-law, reared by two wonderful mothers who have both become my dear friends. And I have two precious grandchildren. Clouds reconfigure into different contours.

Surely, there's cosmic energy bound up in all this somewhere.

AN ELF COMES HOME

Bonnie Frazier

I PUZZLE OVER A SMALL, BUBBLE-WRAPPED ENVELOPE as I sort through today's pile of catalogs and cards. It bears my sister's return address and is surely another Christmas present, though she sent a package just a day or two ago. I toss it on my desk, unsure if it contains a wrapped present or something she expects me to open and wrap for another family member. Later I look more closely and notice words she has scribbled on the back of the envelope: "Not a gift. Open now."

Curious, I open it and shake the contents out on my desk. A folded note and a small plastic elf fall out. No need to read the note. I recognize this elf. I close my eyes and let the long-forgotten memory carry me nearly five decades into the past.

The elf, only two inches tall, stands, or rather sits, in a classic elf-on-a-shelf pose. Most of his painted green elf suit has worn off long ago, leaving him bare and pink. Unembarrassed, he still smiles his saucy smile. I don't remember where I got him, or why I came to have such an elf. The sight of him takes me back to my teen years, before I had my first car. My elf was a key chain fob, attached to my own set of keys to my parents' car. In those carefree days I carried no purse, just my tiny green elf dangling out of a back pocket.

My sister's note says that she is returning the elf to me, that she thinks I'll enjoy having him again. *Ahhh.* And just like that, the rest of the elf-story, the part I had truly forgotten, comes back.

I was about nineteen, preparing to go off to college across the state. Mom kept hinting around about how much she liked my elf. I wasn't really listening, and didn't get what she was trying to tell me. I'd had the elf for several years and it was cute, but so what? Why bring it up now? Eventually, she came out with it: she had a proposition for me, wanted to make a trade. She wouldn't say what it was, but she had something for me, and she'd only give it to me if I gave her my elf in return. The something turned out to be a portable hair dryer, the kind with a hose and a shower cap that girls used in those days, way before hand-held blow dryers, when girls still set their hair on rollers. Oh, yes. A hair dryer would be very useful to have in the dorm. This particular hair dryer, with its slim, stream-lined shape and a carrying handle, was just right for a girl on her way to college. Of course I handed over the elf. I was delighted with

WOMEN'S TRUTHS, WOMEN'S STORIES

my new hair dryer, and Mom purported to be equally delighted with her new elfish key chain.

I'm not sure if Mom really wanted that elf, or she just wanted
a cute way to give me an item she knew I'd need. But the thing
is, she carried that elf for the rest of her life. I never knew her to
have any other key fob. When she died, over forty years later, the
elf was still guarding her keys. I'm surprised my sister remembered it had once been mine.

Someday my children or grandchildren may run across a silly
little green elf, with most of its paint scraped off, tucked away in
a drawer, and they'll wonder why I kept him. All I can say is that
he brought me a sweet memory, and I'm glad he came home.

THINGS AREN'T ALWAYS WHAT THEY SEEM

Bonnie DeMars

CAN YOU BE AMBUSHED BY A WORD?

It happened to me in 1992. I was in relentless pursuit of the
elusive male target. I took aim with video dating, blind dates,
lunch dates, speed dating, and online dating, with no tangible
results. The only winners in the matchmaking games were frustration, disappointment, and bewilderment. I needed a better
tactic to earn a bull's-eye.

I thought I found it. The revered Smithsonian Institution's
lecture series, "The Friday Night Singles Meet and Mingle,"
could be the answer to my prayers. It was a winning combination of educational content and the opportunity to meet a
dating partner. My hopes jumped high.

The first class in the Mid-Atlantic states series focused on the Shenandoah Valley. It attracted a capacity crowd. I arrived early to gain a strategic advantage: scrutiny of male prospects as they entered the lecture hall.

The hour-long, fact-filled, slide-laden lecture seemed endless. Finally, the classroom lights brightened and the matchmaking could begin. We made our way to the reception hall at a snail's pace, not wanting to advertise explicit enthusiasm. I noted no nametags of *Eager* or *Excited* this evening. Alarm set in when I laid eyes on the inauspicious spread: wine like Kool-Aid and meager bites masquerading as hors d'oeuvres. Did this portend the evening's outcome?

I joined an innocuous unit of one unremarkable-looking gal and one average Joe outfitted in office attire. You can get overlooked in a larger gaggle. Dispassionate chatter filled the hall as everyone jockeyed for success.

He entered my peripheral vision and headed straight towards me. Cary Grant he wasn't, but his engaging smile, delicious green eyes, and expressive countenance spoke volumes. He was at least a Tom Hanks. Who could complain about that? And he looked as if he stepped off the pages of GQ. Within moments, Mr. Leading Man landed right next to me and promptly introduced himself to our small group. Wordplay commenced. His charm, wit, age, and height were not lost on me. We settled into pairs.

Looking directly at me, Mr. Charming asked, "Would you like to get some real food?:

Check. This man with shrewd gastronomic sense confirmed my thoughts exactly. The paltry offerings were less than satiating after a long day's work.

"Yes, but I don't have my car."

"No problem, I have mine."

"Okay, let's go."

Right out of the gate, he was a winner. My leading man wanted greener pastures: a real dinner. Before you think I'd taken leave of my senses and good judgment, Mr. Suave and Debonair generated good vibes. I felt reasonably assured I was in no danger. Nothing suggested that he was an ax murderer. If things soured, I had a plan. DC Metro stops are ubiquitous. I could make a hasty escape on public transportation and be home before he realized what happened. We left in search of his car and a better evening.

Our engaging conversation halted only while he opened the car door. Then repartee resumed. Leading Man worked at the IRS. I made a mental note to ask him for some tax pointers. I disclosed that I was in the military. This was my assurance that if he decided to pull any funny business, I could call in the reserves. I'm certain this crossed his mind.

"Have you ever been to the 701?" he asked.

"No, I'm not that familiar with restaurants in downtown DC," I said.

"It's a topless bar," he remarked, with no alteration in his demeanor.

I was stunned! His words stopped me in my tracks. He didn't say that, did he?

It was incongruous that this satisfying package of testosterone would suggest such an outrageous junket. My personal GPS engaged and I zeroed in on my surroundings to register the nearest Metro stop. I was incensed by this apparent subterfuge.

Within minutes we parked the car. I eyed the nearest getaway, but decided to hedge my bets and validate my suspicions. As we approached the door, Mr. Charming opened it with a flourish. We entered the main dining area, a room noticeably absent of neon lights, chrome poles, and loud garish music. Nothing in this establishment fit my mental picture. Was I mistaken or were the tables adorned with linen covers and napkins?

He interrupted my reverie and asked, "Would you prefer a seat at a table or the bar?"

"The bar," I replied like a speeding bullet.

I assured myself that a bar seat guaranteed me a hasty retreat without creating a scene. We headed to the back of the room. Upon reaching our destination, I spied a sleek glass case with tiered shelving loaded with delicious, eye-catching fare.

"What type of tapas would you like?" he asked. All I could do was grin.

I CAN'T BREATHE

Mary Jo Doig

I GREW UP ON THE EASTERN END OF LONG ISLAND, near the Hamptons, in a lower middle-class family of five. When I started school, more than half my classmates were "colored," as we called them in the 1950s. Many were children of Long Island's large migrant population, who worked on the duck and potato farms. The Long Island Railroad ran through our town and those tracks marked the divide between white and black residents' homes. North of the tracks most homes were small, often unkempt shanties that usually had a shiny new car parked in the driveway. The N-word was prevalent and we used to joke about those sparkling clean cars parked in weed-filled yards. The general attitude in my home and community was that black people were second-class citizens and, unfortunately, I believed it.

Despite our financial difficulties, my mother was adamant that I attend college, so I entered an upstate university to become an English teacher. Just a handful of black students attended and I vaguely wondered why. I didn't yet tie that fact to another one: by the time we graduated from high school in 1959, fewer than twenty-five percent of us were black.

As I was journeying into happily-ever-after, working at my degree, marrying my high school sweetheart, becoming the mother of two sons, the dream suddenly shattered when my husband disappeared with another woman. I, not yet degreed, was now a single mother of two small children, with a mortgage, and without a car or income. I got a job I could walk to, but quickly saw that the minimum income would not be enough, so I did the unthinkable: I applied for public assistance for my children. In our town, people on public assistance were in the same boat as colored people: we were second-class, society's leeches, looking for a handout.

I could barely breathe the day I applied for welfare. I felt so shamed, helpless, and angry. In time, I pulled our life back together, returned to college, and completed my degree. Yet I never forgot those eighteen months on public assistance. To this day, I vividly remember standing in lines for government surplus food. Each time my check arrived in my mailbox, my face burned with humiliation.

As it turned out, I never became an English teacher, for having experienced the predicament of my fellow "second-class" peers changed my life. Suddenly I had a passion to help others move ahead in their difficult journeys, as I had been so fortunate to do.

Four years ago, I retired from a varied human services career, where I often met my former self in a new client. The challenge to assist remains and may always be with us, although I strongly hope not. Then last year, when Ferguson and Manhattan blasted to the forefront of our society after the awful, unnecessary killing of unarmed black men, I developed another passionate hope: that our new awareness of avoidable police violence will grow and transform into a movement of restructure, reason, and respect.

I can still hear Eric Garner's voice cry out to the police that he couldn't breathe. In that moment, beyond the tragedy of his death, I also heard him poignantly articulate the plight of all his peers, including myself all those years ago.

When will we *all* be able to breathe?

AN IMAGINED PHONE CONVERSATION

Debra Dolan

Me.   I don't think I am coming out to visit in June.

Mom.   Why not? We are all looking forward to it.

Me.   I thought I was ready.

Mom.   It has been a long time. Does this mean you will never come?

Me.   I never expected to come back. I surprised myself with even putting it forward.

Mom.   I am disappointed.

Me.   I am scared.

Mom.   What scares you?

Me.   That I will feel trapped. That I will feel frightened. That I will feel suffocated. That I will be angry.

Mom.   What do you need from me?

Me.   That I am free to be me. That I can come and go. That I can rest and walk. That I am not on display.

Mom.   I can try but I can't make any promises.

Me.   That is what scares me. That we will both try our best and it won't be good enough. Maybe it is just better that we don't see one another and leave it as before. I want the best for you and hope that you are happy.

Mom.   All I have ever wanted is for you to be happy. Debra, it would make me happy if you came to visit. I have dreamed of this day.

Me.   I feel too much pressure for it to be perfect between us. How can it be? We are strangers to one another.

Mom.   I am your mother.

Long pause . . .

Me.   Why were you not more protective of me? Why did you let that happen? Why did you side with him?

Mom.   I did not know it was happening. He is my husband. When I saw you that morning, so frightened and hurt, I spoke to him. It never happened again.

Me.   I always feared that it would. I'm afraid that I will re-member too much of it in your and his presence, even though it is a different house. I am afraid of the rage that may boil from within. I don't want to be that little scared girl ever again.

Mom.   Please come home. He can't hurt you.

Me.   But you can.

I SHOULD HAVE RAISED MY HAND

Stacy Brookman

AT SEVEN, I KNEW THE ANSWER to Teacher's question, but I didn't raise my hand. I had been taught by my parents to be polite and that showing off to others was a prideful sin. I had also been taught by experience that other kids got mean if they wanted to answer the question and you did, instead. So I let them raise their hands and answer the question in their sinful way. Then they would play with me.

At eighteen, I wanted to go to med school to become a doctor, but I didn't raise my hand. "You should be a secretary and learn dictation," said my soon-to-be. "OK," I chimed. I had been taught that good little wives did what their husbands told them, and I so wanted to be good. Then he would marry me.

At twenty-three, I wanted to go to college and get a degree, and I tried to raise my hand. But he raised his, and put a hole through the door.

At twenty-five, I thought I should raise my hand and say, "It's either her or me!" when I found out, but I didn't. After all, it's impolite to make a big deal about it; forgive and forget is the right thing to do. Then he would stay with me.

At twenty-nine, I knew I should raise my hand and say, "It's either her or me!" but I didn't. It's in the male DNA, they can't help themselves, and I wouldn't want to cause embarrassment for the families, would I? I was the better person for not putting up a fight and just putting the marriage behind me.

At thirty-one, I wanted to raise my hand to point out that quitting your job and moving in with me was quite more than I expected for a two-month relationship, but I didn't. That wasn't hip or cool, and if I did, he might leave and I would be alone again.

At thirty-four, I tried to raise my hand and prevent the big house purchase, but I didn't. His ego would be damaged if I were to point out that he couldn't keep a job. Then he would be insulted and leave.

At thirty-five and thirty-six and thirty-seven and thirty-eight and thirty-nine and forty and forty-one, I should have raised my hand to say, "That's no way to treat our child!" and "That's no way to treat me!" but I didn't. I didn't have it as bad as some, and causing a stir would be, well, selfish of me. Selfishness is a sin, of course.

At forty-two, I finally raised my hand and my head and said, "This has to stop!" and I tried to make him go away. But he wouldn't, and New York courts said they didn't have any proof that I had raised my hand before. So, though I raised my hand and waved and waved, it was in farewell to safety, security, and sanity. I knew I shouldn't have raised my hand.

CAR TOOLS BOXES

Merimée Moffitt

CAR

It's the car sitting in our driveway. The trunk weighed down with extra parts like a lowrider. It's unlocked, and the interior, black leather, has some kind of burly wood details on armrests, the console, and a sexy, creamy-rich smell. I torment myself about having it junked. Yesterday, put my finger in the empty keyhole. Tinted windows make it dark inside. The presidential model Beamer, bulletproof windows. His car. Up on blocks, his fancy hubs and tires were stolen. He cried. Never touched the car again or said a real goodbye. The engine runs; I witnessed the purr. His extra dough was not enough for the trannie. He's gone. Down the rabbit hole filled like those empty mine shafts. Toxic grief: drowning in it, I snap awake. Anger is better. I can pull anger together like silly putty, and apart, make blue weapons or dollhouse furniture, but the grief is liquid and way bigger than me or him or his kids. I have given him six days, as long as it took God to make the world. Six days to get the damned heap out of my driveway. It's broken, he's broken, everyone is broken.

Tools

Arranged like jewels heaped in little steel drawers, tidy cases: needle noses, cutters and claws, grips and wrenches, heavy metal. The sign says, "Hands off! This property protected by angels." I am his angel but I'm not. I carried, set-straight, cleaned, fed, you know, but I can't find a damn angel today. Up to you, the last thing the angels said. All up to you. But writing this reminds me, they're in me. My eyes and hair, everything, my clothes, shopping lists, the soups and salads. Why do I forget and expect them in front of me like jinns, awaiting my wish. Their feathers, long, black, powerful wings, even they are inside me, so old-school. I keep thinking I want drugs, too, but I've tried everything. I climb in, cozy up for the long haul, the ride out of this particular hell, opposite the rabbit hole, a mirrored image high above it all, a carnival juggernaut and it's just me, being me.

Boxes

His stuff inside, what's left of his stuff, lines the walls of my too-big home. The home my other kids arrive to visit, sleep, work, play foursquare, shoot baskets, throw Frisbee in the street, night Frisbee, hot tub soak, club, eat out, catch quick rides to the airport. "Bye Mom, I love you," a sweet memory. 'Cept for him. He is boxes along the wall we ignore. Bathroom stuff, belts, hats, hardhat, photos. Maybe I'll unpack as if box-cutting my veins. Oh, sad to let him go like pulling the plug—cut the cord for God's sake. My parents never kept a thing of mine, not even me. All new territory this holding on tight, tight, tight like the third woman on a whirligig. Centrifugal, no, I won't, I shan't.

THE HOUSE

Jo Virgil

FROM THE DARK BLACK ASPHALT of the newly built road, the farmhouse was barely visible. Even from the sagging cedar and barbed wire gate, a stone's throw from the concrete foundation, it was hard to tell whether the jumble of weathered wood had ever been anything recognizable. But this wonderfully crisp fall day seemed to invite curiosity, so I slipped through the drooping barbed wire and zigzagged my way through the thigh-high grasses and pecan-sized burrs toward a stolen glimpse of someone's past.

I truly was not prepared for the emotional impact of that innocent exploration. I came to feel that I was prying into a stranger's intimate history, peeking at goodnight hugs and eavesdropping on whispered secrets.

The roof of the tiny frame house had caved in almost completely, like a tired old dog collapsed on the ground. Only over the kitchen area was the roof partly intact, but there, one entire wall was gone, its graying boards scattered and piled over what must have once been the side yard, leaving the western sides of two rooms exposed like a giant dollhouse. A steel sink with crudely handmade cabinets on each side was all that identified the kitchen. No furniture, no ornaments, no abandoned boxes of treasures. But still, the house told tales.

The kitchen was tiny, maybe six feet by eight. The design on the wallpaper had long since weathered away and the paint was cracked and peeled. Rows and rows of shelves in the pantry must have once held a bounty of canned goods for the family, maybe homemade in Mason jars. Just behind the kitchen was a small room with one window looking out onto an old oak tree in the yard. The colors of its wallpaper were gone, but the boots-and-cowboy-hat motif spoke volumes. A little boy? Maybe two, sharing the tiny bedroom and learning how to get along?

On the south side of the house, a small square of concrete porch stretched out from the door jamb, welcoming long-ago visitors into the living room, now just a jumble of rotten floorboards and debris. Around the side of the house and towards the back stood what was left of the windmill, its round head of silent blades sadly drooping from the top of the frame, looking like a tired old cowboy. A corral remained mostly intact in the back yard, empty now except for tall weeds and five-foot saplings. Between the corral and the house was the entrance to a storm cellar, doors missing, exposing nothing but darkness and windblown debris.

Nature herself had come to reclaim this piece of land, using her mighty forces of wind and water, sun and ice. The transition was, at the same time, blurrily swift (in geologic terms) and tediously slow (in human terms). I estimated the house to have been built maybe in the 1920s, and probably abandoned with the onslaught of suburban developers in the 1980s.

I could only guess at the more personal history of the home. Had the children grown and left for new homes in different places? Had the parents died, or aged so much that they could no longer care for their home in the country? Had the entire family left in disgust when the rows of tract houses began to block their view of the sunset? Or had a developer offered them more money for their pastureland than they could refuse?

Thirty years ago, this piece of land had been far out in the country, bounded only by country roads and barbed wire, with a clear view of the city skyline twenty miles to the south. On my crisp fall day, the site overlooked two schools and a third under construction, a church, a four-lane divided road, and a sea of brown asphalt shingles atop brick homes.

We call it progress, but doesn't it make you wonder?

THIS LEAVE-TAKING

Sally Nielsen

THE LAST TWO TOMATOES HAVE SHRUNK to squishiness. Dropped brown leaves from my tall ash tree fold into themselves and move into the grandkids' deflated plastic swimming pool. The tree is going bare; the garden is empty. September is the down-sizing month.

Several of my friends have shed their homes and moved into smaller ones, stripping their lives down to the barest house-bone. One moved from a split-level into a smaller house on her new husband's large wooded lot; another built a new house with a forest preserve behind it. Another moved into a cabin in the woods. One moved into the home of a poor Peruvian Andes family now in Guatemala, where she sleeps inside a sleeping bag on a pallet. The leave-takings were tender and sad. But the talk was all about the need for moving on.

One friend desired an ultimate downsizing. She wanted to sell everything, move into one of those one-room homes with only what's needed: a tiny table, tiny bed, and tiny toilet, tucked into tiny corners. She wanted no knickknacks, no neighbors, no rules. She wanted a tiny life.

I wasn't moving anywhere, wasn't desiring to downsize so drastically, but her comments intrigued. So I started looking at YouTube videos of tiny houses built by people who live off-grid. Using the sun, they heat with solar panels attached to their house. They bucket water into the house from an attached cistern. Everything attached to the house is essential.

Life inside a tiny house reminds me of a turtle's life. Everything in the turtle's shell is essential and is attached to the turtle itself. There is no room for anything else. When tiny house dwellers video their spaces, their friendly selfies gaze from inside their shells, two big turtle eyes beam outward, like the headlights of a tiny car.

What does a turtle do when a part of itself is invaded or fails? Does it shed and replace it, like a snake? Or does it downsize and do without, or die? Does it have regret? Three weeks ago, I began to think like a turtle might think.

Doctors had discovered three tiny lumps in my left breast. Tiny cancerous self-invaders. I climbed into my body, eyes first, and watched it for a while, but I could not see them or feel them. In my MRI breast selfie, the invaders appear to be tiny winks inside a tangle of tissues. I wanted to cut them out. But they have taken up too much room and are a type that multiplies.

I am not a turtle. I can downsize myself. I will be shedding two breasts, and replacing them with other parts of my body. I'm not a turtle; I can separate from some parts of my body, leave them behind. I caress my breasts, those old friends, and tell them I will be leaving them in September, moving into a new body, a new life. It is the most intimate and tender of leave-takings.

GROWING

Essays from
Real Women Write

2016

TABLE FOR FIVE

Janice Strohmeier

I CAN FEEL THE MORNING CHILL. I can almost hear the rain slithering down the outside walls, water collecting in tiny pools in the rusted vegetable cans that serve as flowerpots. The sheets, cold and clammy, cling to me. There is nowhere that feels dry.

There's no sun again today. The clouds are thick; I can see them through the small slits of the open bricks at the top of the wall. It's going to be another day of limp laundry hanging on the line begging, waiting desperately for some sun.

I get out of bed and walk over to my dress hanging on the nail hammered into the cement wall. The nail is large and coarse, tiny bits of plaster have chipped away from the wall where the nail met the cement. I dig into my knapsack and find a long-sleeved T shirt that I thought I would need on cool desert nights. There are no cool nights here, what was I thinking? Here, there are just miles and miles of cane fields stretching endlessly before giving way to the grey Gulf waters.

I fold my dress and my T shirt over my arm, tuck my underwear under my armpit, and try to sneak into the bathroom before the kids realize I am awake. The plywood door has rotted in some places. The sides of the door are swollen and the layers of plywood have begun to separate, exposing pale shards of wood that bulge out of the sides. I want to pick at them but I know if I do, the wood will keep peeling back to expose more rot. The hook latch hangs weakly through its eyehole; one good tug would have the latch fall away from the rotting door in a moment of weakness. I hope Mom or Isabel has left the boiler on for hot water this morning.

Before long, I walk into the kitchen to choruses of *good morning auntie, how did you sleep last night, my daughter?* and *sister, did you have enough blankets?* I love these people.

The table is set with plastic placemats and chipped dishes. The placemats have prints of Santa Claus and Rudolph that have faded under several washings with bleach and brush. There are five chairs placed around the table but only two of them match. The table is wobbly and I can see strips of packing tape wound around the tops of the legs to hold in screws that lost their thread some time ago. Cleanly washed and freshly pressed linen napkins sit beside each plate, regally topped by forks with slightly bent tines and tarnished butter knives.

A pitcher of juice sits in the middle of the table. The pitcher used to boast a colorful rooster crowing the morning sun, but the top plume of the rooster has cracked, and most of the plumage has fallen off. Discolored lines now trace the remains of what used to be colorful ceramic feathers. A small wicker basket covered by a worn kitchen towel holds fresh rolls that Isabel bought from the street vendor just moments ago. Mom is at the kitchen counter beside the stove and when she presses a button on the blender, it screams out its defiance against chili peppers, onions, tomatoes, and garlic. The whole concoction sizzles angrily as it hits the hot grease in the frying pan. Underneath it all, fresh eggs burble, promising exquisite *huevos rancheros*. Isabel pours freshly squeezed papaya juice into each of our glasses from the worn-out beak of the rooster. I can see flecks of pulp swirling down to the bottom of my glass.

The kids are freshly showered and they sit brightly at the table, hair plastered back with what I can only imagine is Brylcreem. Caesar smells like a little man; Isabel has dabbed some of Benjamin's leftover cologne on his neck. Iris, with alabaster skin and penetrating onyx eyes framed by massive curls as wild as she is, wilder than her mother ever was, pats the napkin in place on her lap. As she sits erect in her chair, her feet do not touch the ground. Their school uniforms are neatly pressed; the shoulder-crests proudly bear the name of the school. I know Mom woke up in the wee hours to make sure their clothes were ready for school today.

On the floor in the corner of the kitchen is a small charcoal barbecue. It's more of a squat *chiminea* sort of thing, although back then we didn't call them *chimineas* because they weren't yet in fashion. We just needed to heat our home. I think Mom did that for my benefit, my being a foreigner and all. Although a Canadian winter would have killed any Mexican hands-down, I wasn't used to this no-snow-on-the-ground type of winter with dampness permeating everything—clothes, books, bedsheets, walls. Your soul.

The smoke rising up from the burning hunks of coal, white and glowing under the grate of the chiminea, pierces my nose. In any other kitchen in my former reality, the smoke would have clogged the room, choked the breath out of us. However, in this kitchen, the courtyard doors are open and the airshaft seems to beckon the smoke up and out into the morning sky.

The kids are arguing about who got their homework completed first last night, and whose new knapsack is the prettiest. Whose will be the envy of the school? The new knapsacks with their Made-in-Canada maple leaf symbol are sure to raise eyebrows in all the classrooms at school, not just first and third grades. As the kids roll their beans into homemade freshly-warmed tortillas and scoop their scrambled eggs in wide mouthfuls, Mom walks over to the table and pours hot, thick coffee into my mug. The faint scent of cinnamon rises up in tiny swirls around my nostrils.

The day has begun.

ORDINARY DAYS

Susan Wittig Albert

Who would live happily in the country must be
wisely prepared to take great pleasure in little things.
— Henry Beston

THE BEST DAYS BEGIN ABOUT 6:30 A.M., waking from a warm dream to a kiss from my husband and an ecstatic canine greeting. (The cat is not particularly affectionate, except with Bill.) Make the bed, brew fresh coffee, start a load of laundry. Coffee in hand, turn on the computer, check the e-mail for urgencies, glance at the weather radar and the front page of the online *New York Times.* And then out with the dogs.

Eighteen degrees this January morning, the frost a bright, brittle crust of diamonds on grass, weeds. It is just dawn, and the three dogs and I walk the east meadow loop: across the field to the Ramsey Ranch fence; along a path under live oaks, cedars, and mesquite; up the lane behind the abandoned barn to the pasture where our cows and sheep stand broadside to the winter sun, warming their brown flanks. The dogs delight in the trace scents of the deer, coons, possums, mice, and coyotes that travel this same path every night (it's their territory, too, their homeland, their place). As I walk, I revel in the sights and sounds of this very ordinary place—the cardinals flashing scarlet through the dark green junipers, the frostbitten grasses of our remnant scrap of native prairie, the lamentations of mourning doves.

Thirty minutes later, I'm back in the kitchen making pancakes, golden, crunchy with Bill's pecans. We gathered an astonishing two hundred pounds last fall from the trees he's grafted and cultivated. We won't run out of pecans for a while. And then the day's ordinary work: a casserole out of the freezer for supper; laundry into the dryer, another load into the washer; a quick sweep of the kitchen floor (oh, the dog fur!). Then I'm on my way back to the computer to finish the e-mail, post to the blog, make an entry in this journal, and open the file on the writing project that will keep me busy the rest of the workday.

Late in the afternoon, Bill and I drive up to the barn to break the ice on the tank that supplies water for Texas and Blossom, our longhorn cows, and Mutton, a Barbados sheep. I feed the animals their wintertime ration of cow cake, chopped corn, and sorghum and molasses, and scatter corn for the ducks and the pair of large white ganders we call Mutt and Jeff. The seven white and four black ducks were released on our little lake last summer by a neighbor and were adopted by Mutt and Jeff, who clearly needed something to do besides swimming and eating. These two big ganders take their parenting duties seriously, herding their unruly charges with a nip here, a tuck there, an occasional wing-swat. Little things, as Henry Beston says. Fun to watch.

I love living here at Meadow Knoll, the name we gave to this patch of Texas Hill Country when we came here in 1986. It is a small, ordinary, thirty-one acre stretch of meadows and woods on the east side of a variable-level lake that was scooped out in the early 1970s by a small-time developer with overblown ideas and an oversized bulldozer. The lake is fed by a spring, a creek, and rainwater runoff from a 400-acre watershed. Full, it covers about twenty acres. During droughts (like the one we're living through now), it can shrink to the size of a wading pool. Before white settlers arrived, the area was the site of a Tonkawa Indian campground—perhaps a trade camp, where Tonkawa, Caddo, and Jumano came together to swap goods and food and news. The road to the lake is called Indian Wells, reflecting the old-timers' knowledge of the campsite.

If there were any archaeological remains at the Indian Wells spring, that fool with the bulldozer chewed them up. Pity. Researchers in nearby counties have uncovered human-occupied campsites dating back some twelve thousand years. For centuries, the Hill Country was home to a network of peaceable hunter-gatherer families, clans, and tribes, moving north and south, east and west, in the regular pursuit of deer and bison and seasonal harvests: pecans, mesquite beans, prickly pear cactus. All this changed in the mid-1800s when the fierce Comanches attacked from the north and the land-hungry Anglos pushed in from the east. Together, they squeezed out the friendly, trusting, transient Tonkawas.

But I think of the Tonks often, especially on nights when the moon is full. I imagine them camped at the spring, on the sloping hill, relaxing beside their fires or asleep in tipis and brush huts. Sometimes I think: if I look hard enough, maybe I'll see them, see their spirits or the drifting smoke from their campfires, hear the barking of camp dogs, the singing of the children—the ordinary pleasures of a peaceful life. But they're gone, extinct now or nearly so, their homeland carved into ranches and farms and subdivisions. In place of their camp, a developer's lake: home to herons, kingfishers, migrating cormorants, Mutt and Jeff, a flock of unruly ducks. And us.

The early evening twilight is settling like a gray scarf across the landscape, and we are driving home. Home, where Bill lights a fire in the fireplace while I feed the dogs. The casserole is ready to come out of the oven, and a book is waiting for me to open it for a few hours' reading. It's been a good day, and I remember Henry Beston. "Who would live happily in the country must be wisely prepared to take great pleasure in little things," he says.

Little things, great pleasure. Yes, I think he's right.

KITCHEN REVOLUTION

Penelope Starr

TWISTY CLEAR PLASTIC AIRLOCKS jut out of the tops of mason jars filled with canary yellow and bluish purple sauerkraut. A jar with a perforated top is tilted face-down in a stainless steel bowl, so mung bean sprouts can drain. A hand-woven cotton dishtowel is draped over the opening of a two-gallon glass jug, where kombucha and its starter "mother" reside, turning tea and sugar into a fermented powerhouse of healthy organisms. Yogurt is warmly tucked in its blanket at 110 degrees, waiting for *lactobacillus acidophilus* to do its magic. Sourdough bread proofs in a warm corner on the counter. My kitchen looks more like a science lab than a food preparation area. Bottles and containers, strainers and graters, these are the tools I am using to heal myself.

Over five years ago, I started to cough. It began with frequent throat clearings and an occasional burst of dry hacks that quickly turned violent. Great breath-stealing, rib-busting spasms became more frequent until I ended up in Urgent Care attached to a breathing machine. I was sent home with a prescription for an inhaler for my next emergency and no answers about why this was happening to me. Soon, the spaces between my coughing fits got closer and I developed a strange wheeze that was audible across a room. Being horizontal brought on the fiercest attacks so sleeping became a challenge.

I dragged myself to a succession of experts looking for a cure. I had x-rays to check for valley fever and allergy tests to find out that everything that grows outside is my enemy. I bought prescription nose sprays and a neti pot, B vitamins, Claritin, and Nyquil. Nothing helped. Acupuncture, aromatherapy, Reiki, yoga, mindfulness and meditation: I tried them all with disappointing results.

Being in public was challenging. On airplanes, I felt compelled to assure my seatmates that I was not contagious, I just coughed. During meals, conversations stopped when my face turned a deep crimson and it looked like I was choking on my last bite. I became the focus of attention in social situations, when the cough would prompt at least one person to offer the Heimlich maneuver. I politely declined in pantomime because the cough precluded me from speaking.

I read many books on how to heal myself with food and found that one possible cause of the cough was "silent GERD," or a type of acid reflux that bypassed the typical heartburn and landed in my throat. I had medical procedures that probed the tubes that make up my digestive system from both ends. I began to follow a GERD diet. I learned to love the previously despised fennel and gave up chocolate and peppermint. My one concession to the medical monopoly was a small purple pill that I took every morning before breakfast.

My quest for a solution led me to Sandor Katz, an enthusiastic lover of all things fermented and author of *The Art of Fer-*

mentation. His life's work is being validated by a raft of current scientific studies, which declare that you are not only what you eat but also what's living inside your gut. According to research, having the correct microbiota can make you healthier, smarter, calmer, and thinner.

Finally, I was getting some results. Regular exercise, smaller meals, drinking lots of pure water, ingesting whole foods and all kinds of fermented foods seemed to do what none of the doctors could do for me. I stopped taking the purple pill.

I still suck on a lot of cough drops, and am occasionally wakened by a coughing attack, but I am slowly getting better. My gut is happy and that makes me happy.

I have had a few relapses. Collective wisdom says that booze irritates GERD, but occasionally a glass of chilled white wine beckons me. As does a garlic and sundried tomato pizza. Sometimes I think that I'm too busy to go to the gym. Old patterns are hard to break, but when the discomfort and coughing come back, I take it as a reminder that I am in charge of my own health and I do what I need to do to heal myself. I head into the kitchen and check on my science experiments.

Author Michael Pollan says, "To reclaim control over one's food, to take it back from industry and science, is no small thing; indeed, in our time, cooking from scratch qualifies as subversive." The revolution has already started in my kitchen.

WAKING UP

Mary Lee Fulkerson

I TAPPED THE BRAKE as a jackrabbit scrambled across the road. Back in 1985, Highway 50 was a lonesome Nevada road, where eagles and hawks swooped to feast on critters like the one that just got away. In the passenger seat, Kathleen, my partner in this formidable mission, slept blissfully on. I pursed my lips in a quiet whistle, feeling a little defiant, a little scared, and a little proud.

We were doing it! This 300-mile trip to the Duckwater Indian reservation was a long time coming. Kathleen and I, genuine products of the 1950s generation, were striking out on our own.

Until recently our role was clear: keep the house clean, serve a well-balanced meal at six, and support our husbands and children. In any spare time, we sought little part-time jobs and volunteered here and there. The Women's Movement came along in time to embolden our daughters, but we never dreamed it would catch up and run right over us, too. Betty Friedan's *The Feminine Mystique* and Gloria Steinem's *Ms.* magazine riveted us. Why couldn't a woman be a mailman, they asked? And if so, she would be called a "mail carrier" (that term shocked us). Why couldn't she be a lawyer or college professor or a road flagger, or anything a man could be? We were first horrified at these ideas, then mystified, and finally we embraced feminism. This, our magical road to freedom, was long and rocky, and is grist for many hilarious and heart-wrenching stories, but the idea that we could actually direct our own lives changed us forever.

I finished college at forty-eight and met Kathleen; together we built our careers as professional basket artists. One day, we learned that Native American basketry here in the Great Basin was the longest continuing basket tradition in the United States, and few people were aware of it.

Kathleen and I knew baskets. Knew the hours and days spent gathering and preparing materials, knew the skill required. We also felt that native people, like women, were an under-appreciated fragment of the human race.

We decided right there to write a book about these native basket makers, and embarked upon an odyssey we thought would take a few months, but which stretched into years. Kathleen learned the mysteries of a camera and I bought my first computer, both amazingly complicated instruments. We needed to gain the weavers' confidence, but first we had to use our newfound skill of reading road maps and find the weavers, who lived in nooks of sand and sage all over the Great Basin. And I needed to write it all down in an interesting yet factual style. And—oh, yeah—we had to find a publisher.

We accomplished all that, rubes that we were. And now here we were, approaching the little town of Eureka, where we would return to spend the night after interviews. I woke Kathleen. It was already late afternoon as I pulled into the gas station and proudly pumped my own gas, another new accomplishment. "How far to Duckwater?" I asked the attendant.

" 'Nother twenty miles." He looked at my 1985 Buick doubtfully. My husband, Chuck, had insisted we take the new car to reduce the chance of automotive problems.

"How's the road?" I asked.

"Fine,'til you get to the turnoff. Then watch out. Rocks all the way in. This here's your last gas station."

The assertive woman (me) jumped in the Buick and hit the road, gravel flying. We needed to conduct an interview and return before dark. Kathleen leaned forward. "Let's hope Evelyn got our message." Evelyn Pete was the Shoshone weaver we were to visit. She had no phone and we'd never met, but through a series of messages called the "Indian grapevine," we thought we had a date for three p.m. People said we couldn't miss her house. It was now four, and I had never maneuvered through so many rocks. I stepped on the gas pedal.

The tire went down.

We were miles from everywhere, on a strange road, headed for a house with no address, as daylight dimmed. We retrieved the tire-changing directions and read that this model required a certain key to reach the spare. I had no key.

In the distance, a little road branched off and a stand of cottonwoods indicated a nearby house. Kathleen, refreshed from her sleep, said, "I'll find someone!" and she dashed down the road, soon disappearing from view. I waited. Read my notes. Searched for the spare tire key. Contemplated women's lib. Finally, a ribbon of fine dust signaled the approach of a car. It stopped and Kathleen and two young Shoshone men jumped out. One, who said he was Mitch Pete, Evelyn's son, looked at my spare area with confidence.

"It'll be fine," he smiled. His friend Joe drove us back down the road and stopped at a house nestled against the cottonwoods. Evelyn's house.

We could hardly contain our wonder at the sight unfolding in Evelyn's back yard. She sat in an old lawn chair under a leafy cottonwood, weaving a great burden basket, her willows soaking in the clear stream and a winnowing basket of pine nuts at her feet. Mitch's beaded pipe-in-progress lay against a nearby rock. Evelyn's brother, Bud, smoothed a stone down the shaft of a spear. A rabbit fur blanket hung over a rope clothesline and swayed in the breeze.

We had discovered a paradise in the middle of the Nevada desert. That vision, those kind and smart people, that way of life, became our guiding light as we devoted the next years to finding more basket weavers on Nevada reservations, recording their stories, purifying in sweat lodges, learning about a culture that carried the tradition of their ancestors onward into the new century.

The South American writer Antonio Machado described in one sentence what I could not say in this entire story. "Beyond living and dreaming there is something more important: waking up."

BECOMING AN
ELDER OF THE EARTH
Deborah Doblado Bowers

ASLEEP FACE DOWN ON A SMALL WOVEN RUG at the base of a lone pine tree, near a rippled lake and a grassy meadow, I feel the Earth shake. A single strong jolt awakens me. Startled, I look up to see Earth Dancer, a large male buffalo, one of three American bison moving around my vision circle since early morning. He is approximately twenty feet away, standing in the direction of the South, calmly grazing on patches of green grass. It seems I have been oblivious to him.

Did the movement of the buffalo make the Earth shake? The jolt was strong enough to wake me from the sound sleep I so desperately seek. I ask aloud, "Did you shake the Earth, or did the Earth shake Herself?" The answer lies in his silent walk in the direction of the West. Am I in a dream state or is this waking reality? I feel the vibration in my bones, in my body still. Prostrate upon the Earth, I contemplate these questions a while longer. No matter the source, the message is clear. Wake up and pay attention!

Hawk calls loudly again and again. Red bird points the way. My fasting body is exhausted. Sleep is short and disturbed. A thin, sky-blue woolen shawl from India covers me, a remembrance from my days of following a guru. I wear it like a shroud, covering my body as I lay upon the Earth; the sky is visible through the arms of the pine tree with its pregnant cones aplenty. The day is sunny and warm, with coolness hidden in the strong wind blowing across the meadow, causing ripples on the surface of the lake. The position of the sun tells me it is late afternoon. It is a sensual path.

I am here at Deer Dancer Ranch in Texas, the site of years of sacred ceremonies. The roots of my relationship with the Medicine Wheel take hold on this land, within the nature-based spiritual community of the Earthtribe. At fifty-eight, it is my first time to make a vision quest. At this point in the story, it has been a year since I put my stake in the ground, committing myself to a focused time with Spirit, vision guidance and preparation. I learn the vision quest is a tool, a doorway to enter spiritual realms, revealing a direction for life. It is a time to retreat into nature in solitude, providing an opening to a heightened state of awareness. My mentor informs me the vision I seek is on behalf of the tribe as well as myself.

Two years earlier, I began attending a monthly sweat lodge ceremony, where people gather to deepen their spiritual lives and reconnect to Mother Earth. It is a healing process. I joined a study in spiritual mentoring with Earthtribe founders Dr. Will Taegel and Dr. Judith Yost. I learned the Wheel can be used as a map, a guiding tool for life. I know it as an ancient symbol used by Native Americans. In the fall, at the annual Earth Dance, I help to lead the direction of the East, a place of birthing new beginnings. It is a time of deep reflection on our relationship to the Earth, through creativity, dance, and laughter. All the while,

I find my relationship with the Earth is being reborn. Questing and ceremonial practice deepen the connection, helping me move beyond my comfort zone.

On the early morning walk to my vision site, two supporters guide me. We are astonished to find three buffalo along the path. A little later, sitting alone inside my vision circle of 405 multi-colored prayer bundles, Earth Dancer approaches directly from the North, the place of masculine energy, courage, strength and focus. The voice of Changing Buffalo, a tribal elder, whispers in my ear, "If a buffalo approaches, stand tall and firm upon the Earth, with arms raised and feet wide, do not draw near, respect its wildness, and ask permission to spend time on this land." Grateful for the memory of this wise counsel, I do as instructed, allowing the energy of this act to feed me.

My body is framed and supported by the pine tree at my back. The companionship of this tree instills strength and comfort, helping me to find my voice. I tell Earth Dancer I am here to listen to any message he may have for me. When I ask him to respect his distance, not to come too close, not to come inside my vision circle, he stops and turns away as though he understands.

The powerful yet gentle presence of these grand creatures of nature, moving sun wise—gradually, cautiously, and deliberately—around my vision circle, shifts me into an altered state of consciousness. The feeling of a safe container is created, safe enough for me to awaken to their teaching of the wheel, in what I would come to understand later as preparation for a lesson in soul retrieval, the act of healing a hidden, traumatic wound.

When the Earth shakes me awake in the vulnerable and compassionate arms of the South, I become aware the buffalo are greeting me in an up-close-and-personal way at each of the four cardinal directions of the Medicine Wheel: North, East, South, and West. This guiding wheel of buffalo surrounds the safe circle of colorful prayer ties, providing an extra cushion of protection, filling me with the courage to enter the dark, shadowy teaching of the West, and face the unfinished business of my youth. This experiential lesson of the buffalo roots itself deeply within the womb of my being, providing an intimate map on how to walk the Medicine Wheel—slow, steady, and focused. The nature name bestowed on me for this quest is *Buffalo Wheel.*

THE BLOCK PARTY

Maya Lazarus

A SUMMERTIME EVENT IN 1955: our annual Joralemon Street block party in Brooklyn Heights. Shouts and cheers from the crowds at the game booths. I smell onions and peppers frying, to eat with spicy sausages. Popcorn sounds like firecrackers as it jumps and sizzles. I stare in amazement at the wheel-like machine spinning pink cotton candy. My dad hands me the sticky stuff on a paper stick and shoos me off down the crooked sidewalk. I can hear Mom chattering with our next-door neighbors and our tenants, Jean and Marian. Her voice steadies me. I'm alone, but not alone, as she catches my attention and smiles. My sister, Donna, two years older, is roaming somewhere. I couldn't care less about what she's doing. She never has time for me. Pinches me when no one is looking. I can run in the street if I want to because the traffic is blocked off.

I cross over to Willow Place. The shadowy trees along the sidewalk send me back. I already see shapes moving behind those trees. I turn around and skip across the cobblestones and stand with my back to our row house, looking out at the street think-ing, "This is the best night of my life!" Around my feet lie gum wrappers, greasy waxed papers that once wrapped around hot dogs, empty cotton candy sticks with beads of sweetness cling-ing, and Popsicle sticks still wet. People's voices are rising on top of each other. The party is in full swing.

Suddenly, my dad taps me on my shoulder and I look up, barely making out his face in the streetlight glare. He's holding his white handkerchief over one eye. I wonder where his glasses are. In the calmest of voices, amid the din, he says, "Tell your mom I'm going to the hospital. A boy broke my glasses with a dart, and I think there's a piece of glass in my eye." I have an im-mediate image of his eye bleeding and cut up, but I can't see the blood because he's covered his eye with the handkerchief. I don't know what to say. I feel my stomach toss about. I'm scared. But Dad's touch and the squeeze to my shoulder reassure me that everything will be OK. It always is.

You Have to Be Carefully Taught

Ethel Lee-Miller

CAN YOU REMEMBER THE DIZZYING FEELING of your first love? I know how trite that sounds, like the loopy writing in a teenager's diary with a little heart over each *i*. But I can remember, I really can. And I was only recently past being a teenager, so why not the dizzy feeling?

I danced into the kitchen where my sisters and I had curtsied and twirled as little girls in front of the refrigerator, to the delight of our parents. Now I felt light enough to rise up and float over my mother's head as she moved through a week's worth of ironing for our family. When I bounced back down to the linoleum floor, I swirled around the ironing board, trailing my fingers along the sleeve of Dad's office shirt.

My mother looked up, resting the iron with a clunk on the metal pad, caught for three seconds in the joy that was shooting from me. Then back to the ironing.

"He called." I sighed, with all the trust and joy a twenty-year-old wrapped in infatuation could emit in two words.

"Who?" came my mother's muffled voice as she bent over the ironing board.

"Malachi. He works at the plant. He has the gentlest voice and is just gorgeous."

"Malachi? What kind of a name is that?"

"It's from the Bible. I looked it up. It means prophet or messenger, and his message is he wants to take me out to the movies."

I laughed and actually hugged myself. This was just too delicious.

"He's really tall—six-feet-seven. He has the most beautiful smooth skin. His arms look like silky dark chocolate."

"Do you mean he's a Negro?" My mother's voice held an unmistakable incredulous tone, tinged with some hostility.

"Well. Yes, he's black, Mom." My spin was slower. "What's the matter with that?"

"Friends, okay," was the flat reply. "But not to go on dates." She clunked the iron down again and walked out of the kitchen.

I'm always amazed at the power and speed of memory. In the time it took my mother to disappear into her bedroom, I saw many past images. My mother separating from her father's prejudice by opening our summer home as a vacation place for children of different racial backgrounds. My mother piling boxes of clothes and food into cartons, and driving the cartons, along with my sister and me as witnesses, to deliver to a black family that lived in a shed in the middle of a farm field. I saw my neighbors tally up signatures and arrange for buses for the March on Washington in 1963. I remembered litanies of equality from my childhood. *Everyone is equal. No name-calling.*

With all the innocence of a child, I believed that these actions went straight from intellectual decisions to behavior, to moral fiber that wove its way into matters of the heart.

The iron was hissing. I automatically reached out and turned it off. My heart was still beating far too fast, not from euphoria, but from the realization that what I thought was the cross-my-heart-and-hope-to-die truth was simply ... not. And I didn't know why.

The world stopped spinning.

Musings from the distance of time are sometimes more objective, more balanced with maturity and the willingness to step into someone else's shoes. Perhaps my mother could have explained that surface behaviors are not always grounded in core beliefs. Perhaps I could have hinted at a new friend, then developed him into a new crush, then delivered the skin pigmentation issue. But I was twenty and she was fifty, both of us products of our ages and the times.

LONG-AGO ROMANCE

Marian McCaa Thomas

WHEN YOUR BOYFRIEND WEARS FULL-LENGTH LEG BRACES because he had polio, his lap is not the most comfortable place to sit!

Still, the right circumstances can make even the uncomfortable appealing. He was a senior in college, and I was a year behind. I knew he would be going to graduate school thousands of miles away, and we would not be able to see each other for many months. Naturally, we wanted to take advantage of being in the same place as often as we could. Our college campus, however, didn't provide many places where one could find privacy for romance. The director of the campus YWCA was well aware of this limitation, and she offered to let us use her apartment off-campus for a rendezvous.

"Go ahead, cook him a meal, relax, and enjoy a quiet evening together," she said as she handed me the key. She undoubtedly trusted me, the student president of the YWCA, to behave myself. On the chosen day, a day she was out of town, I went to her place to cook and set the table for two. As I did so, I imagined what it would be like if we were married, and I'd be cooking dinner and anticipating his coming home from work.

When he arrived at the apartment, we enjoyed eating together and talking without the noisy chatter of the dormitory dining room where we usually ate. After cleaning up the kitchen, we put on some music and continued our conversation. He was sitting in a chair that looked strong enough to hold us both, so when he beckoned me to join him there, I gingerly sat on his lap. Our clothes gave some padding between his leg braces and my bottom, and as soon as we began kissing, my sensations were concentrated elsewhere. We were blissfully enjoying those leisurely kisses when a loud knock on the door made us jump. He pushed me off his lap, a rather guilty look on his face. I slowly opened the door and found a neighbor asking for Gladyce.

"She's out," I apologized, and quickly shut the door. The romantic mood was broken, and we reluctantly decided to leave our temporary sanctuary. The memory of that evening, however, still brings a smile to my face, even after more than fifty-three years of marriage to the same man who held me in his lap.

STRIPPER

Carol Ziel

I STEPPED OUT OF THE DARKNESS and into the neon lights. Finally, I had come home. Rooted to the beer-soaked carpet, I stood in a moment of Resurrection. Like Lazarus rising from the dead, I came alive. Scales fell from my eyes and I saw absolute beauty and freedom. The stage was above me—a shrine to womanhood, and I had finally found my place in the world.

I had never truly seen a woman's body before. Raised in a convent for many years, T shirts and cotton bras were the norm—never tassels or pasties. We had three-minute showers to discourage familiarity with our bodies. My faith tradition taught me that the body was a source of evil. But here was Eve before the Fall, revealing the possibility of who I might be as a woman. An exotic dancer became my mentor.

I returned to that club for many months and sat at the edge of the stage—I and a string of adoring men, pockets full of dollars. I was mesmerized by her movement, her grace. No shame, no embarrassment, no apologies for being female—just celebration through dance. Celebration through her flexibility, openness, boldness, and sense of humor. She was as comfortable in a modified stewardess's or firefighter's uniform as in her street clothes, and she reveled in the process of revealing herself. What I brought to the edge of her stage was my own history of sexual trauma and my own thwarted connection to my body. I was hoping for healing. Maybe at least, osmosis would gift me with the freedom and acceptance that I saw in her.

Each week I returned to memorize her movements. Eventually the edge was not enough and I wanted to be up there with her. I wanted to be absorbed into her energy, her ambiance, her very person, and experience that freedom. I wanted to be part of her grace and sensuality. I wanted to burst from my cocoon and merge with this creature who spread her wings like a butterfly. I wanted to be her.

My time did come. There was a side stage for neophytes. I stood at the bottom and waited my turn. The woman before me was in her fifties. She was wooden, jerking like a robot, eyes as flat and blank as Little Orphan Annie's. Something inside of me shifted. I looked at her husband, who was drooling and vacant. All of the men around me were slack-faced and wild-eyed. They were not who I imagined them to be in the beginning—temple priests worshipping a priestess. Once again the scales fell. This time I saw a different story.

WOMEN'S WISDOM: THE PAPER TRAIL

Connie Spittler

WOMEN BELONG TO AN ANCIENT TRIBE of storytellers, a long line of ancestors who washed clothes down by the river and remembered, who sewed at quilting bees and talked of the past, cooked for harvesters and shared stories, held children on warm laps and whispered true tales. Today, in laundromats and spas, or texting on coffee breaks, women talk of life's unfolding events to one another. No matter where it happens, this is storytelling, one of our oldest traditions. As writers, we pursue the stories worth telling and find reasons enough to write the words down, producing a testament to the fact that we were here.

Poet Muriel Rukeyser asked, "What would happen if one woman told the truth about her life?" Her answer: "The world would split open." Because of the universal knowledge we hold within us, telling it, sharing it, writing it down sets the commotion in motion. Like a breakfast egg, we crack open the sphere that is our world and find our truth, the simple wisdom that comes from life stories.

Since time eternal, women have passed on wisdom. We've told and retold family stories as we stirred the soup, wiped little noses, and comforted oldsters. Never mind that we've accomplished some other great things: led countries, discovered radium, protected the environment, founded colleges, and crusaded against birth defects. Think of Indira Gandhi, Marie Curie, Rachel Carson, Mary Mc-Leod Bethune, and Virginia Apgar, M.D., to name a few.

But closer at hand, we soothe teething babies and clean mineral deposits off faucets. We make paste from flour and water in the morning and gravy thickener from water and flour in the afternoon, working from common knowledge and passed-on wisdom.

When a friend calls for advice, a class needs teaching, the gravy is too thin, we contribute our knowledge and skill. Life turns these corners into experience. We turn these corners into stories offering a tantalizing mix of information—family stories, homey postscripts, heartbreaking secrets, like the reason cousin Maria doesn't talk to cousin Elena, or how to remove film off pots and pans with pickle juice, or our medical family history of miscarriage, or reasons I was beaten as a child by Daddy.

When we're too busy mopping our floors or our brows to write our stories, valuable information is lost, words and phrases left crumbled in the dust. How was the family name pronounced in the old country? Why did Gramma take medication? How did Aunt Rose's fiancé die in World War II? Who was the original owner of the gold pocket watch in the bureau drawer?

Women carry this practical, historical, emotional wisdom within. It flutters near the surface of our awareness and if we feel so inclined, we part with it. We write it down. In my family, with technology, the old family tales lost their sheen. My mother dismissed Gramma's time and ways. She didn't want to discuss the Great Depression or steep ginger for nausea. She preferred new appliances, pharmacy prescriptions, and cake mixes. Fortunately, ideas recycle. Like healing herbs and chicken soup, we can reclaim the tradition of telling our old-fashioned stories, bringing them into contemporary life. Whether we are thirty or one hundred, passing on the things we've learned has never been so important.

As storywriters, there are common things and things-in-common. Bundling up our hopes and dreams, we find creative joy, whether the increment is word, paragraph, page, or chapter. Board by board, wall by wall, we build something of our own making. As we read the words of others, we understand that every woman's life, every woman's contribution, counts as heavily as the next. The words of the cleaning woman are as important as those of the business executive. Each lives in a story house of wisdom, possessing personal knowledge to be made available to others.

Remember Muriel Rukeyser's question, "What would happen if one woman told the truth about her life?" My mind visualizes the earth as it reacts ever so gently to one woman who begins her story and unfolds her reality. Then the world reverberates to the creative buzzing of another, then hundreds, no thousands, why not millions of women, speaking out, telling the truth of their lives. The globe moves to the magnificent hubbub of happiness, sadness, love, laughter, grieving, and anger, as women's words sing out, each story separate, yet each story connected by a mystical thread reaching back to ancient times.

I imagine their words on paper and when the stories are written, the sphere trembles in anticipation as the pages go flying round and round, faster and faster, spinning and turning, cream into butter, egg white to meringue, straw into gold, life into stories—until Mother Earth splits open from the pure joy of it all.

As we rotate a ball of truth around and about in the palm of our hand, others await our truth, the mystical lore, inexplicable bits and pieces of data, facts and tales handed down from relative to relative.

You know only one part for sure, your own, rolled together from knowledge carried forward from centuries ago. Add to this the things you've learned in all the yesterdays of your lifetime, traveling from there to here. You hold the measure of universal knowledge in your grasp, the symbolic breakfast egg. It is this certain wisdom that makes things happen, a world spinning more smoothly in its orbit because of women working at their tasks. The simple and dramatic things they do. Take up your pencil and paper. Get out your typewriter. Turn on your computer. Get ready to crack open your world.

When the writing is finished, then say, "Yes, I was here." Your stories will last as long as the paper that holds them.

Long live this endless paper trail of women's wisdom.

About the Contributors

Susan Wittig Albert is the author of memoirs, mysteries, historical fiction, and nonfiction. She has been published by several traditional publishers and also publishes her work under her own imprint, Persevero Press. Susan founded SCN in 1997 and is currently (2015-2017) serving as its president. She and her husband Bill live in the Texas Hill Country.

Linda Austin became an advocate for lifewriting after writing her mother's memoir of growing up in Japan around WWII.

Pat Bean is a retired, award-winning journalist, who spent nine years traveling this country in a small RV with her canine companion, Maggie. You can read all about her adventures in *Travels with Maggie,* and on her blog. She is an avid birdwatcher and nature enthusiast. Pat has five children, 15 grandchildren, and five great-grandchildren. She now lives in Tucson with her canine companion Pepper. http://patbean.wordpress.com

Joyce Boatright is a writer, storyteller, and teacher, who finds this life-journey an extraordinary experience. She teaches expressive writing for reflection and personal growth at the Carl Jung Education Center in Houston, and serves on the Story Circle Network Board as Program Chair.

With a love of travel, **Deborah Doblado Bowers** and her husband chose to live and work globally through the Federal Civil Service. They raised three sons, exploring cultures in the Philippines, Cuba, Spain, and USA. In between changing diapers and mending cuts, Deborah earned a BS in Liberal Arts, was a Federal employee, administered a transitional supportive homeless project, and taught prevention programs. Retired in Wimberley,

TX, she began a nature-based spiritual journey, learning that a path to wholeness is inextricably tied to ones relationship with Earth. To deepen the process, she became a Master Naturalist, completed a Masters degree and a Doctor of Ministry in Wisdom Spirituality. Deborah's love of the arts has taken her into writing, photography, assemblage art, and Qigong.

Stacy Brookman wants to live in a world where everyone feels free to share their stories…and listeners gain wisdom from them. She interviews fascinating people on Real Life Resilience podcast, the culmination of years working to understand the psychology and the art of lifestory writing, making it easy for others to write their stories. Her latest project is a webinar – 4 Simple, Proven Methods to Writing the First Chapter of Your Life Story in Just 7 Days. As a proponent of life storytelling as a means of healing from trauma, Stacy has been featured on many podcasts and speaks at selected events. She enjoys sharing ways to discover your life theme, write through difficulties, and become a more resilient person. Find Stacy at www.stacybrookman.com/webinar.

Born in Missoula, **Karen Buley** credits her roots to Butte, Montana, the birthplace of her parents and her home throughout much of her childhood. She is the author of the novel, *Nanny on the Run*. Her collection of nurses stories, *Nurses on the Run: Why They Come, Why They Stay*, was chosen a "Best Books 2010" Awards finalist by USA Book News. A former contributor to Working Nurse and Nursetogether.com, Karen's essays have appeared in Family Circle, American Nurse Today, and *A Cup of Comfort for Nurses: Stories of Caring and Compassion*. After years of obstetrical nursing, Karen traded the magic of birth for the magic of books and now works as a high school library assistant in Missoula.

Lois Ann Bull discovered at 50 that she's a raconteur with a good memory and a love of writing. Now at 76, she says, "I still have thousands of tales to tell. Something triggers a mental picture and the stories bubble up. Even I am amazed by what I remember. It's a far cry from texting and talking with emojis. I self-published three books for my family and am working on a fourth and fifth. I had no idea I'd have so much fun as an elder. My husband and I live in Connecticut in a household managed by a Black Labrador Retriever and a Seal Point Siamese (rescued). My friends call me Lois, my grandkids call me Lolo, and my husband calls me Lovey."

Stephanie Dalley was "born and raised on the East Coast—a real Jersey Girl! Once I completed High school, I went into Manhattan and attended FIT, which led to all kinds of opportunities career-wise. I have two children. Molly, the oldest, lives on the West Coast, and my son Ryan lives on the East. Years passed, kids grew up, I realized I was powerless to alcohol and any other substance, got well, worked in the field of alcohol and recovery, and met my soul mate, who was also working at the same facility. After a year we got married, he was one of those "roses on the table" every week guys. Never looked at another woman and brought me ten years of happiness. Then they discovered stage 4 cancer, aggressive, inoperable. The MDs said, 'do your bucket list now, you have less than 9 months to live,' and he stood up and said, 'I'm not going anywhere, I love my wife too much.' "The Third Night" was written during that time."

Barbara Dee is the co-founder of Suncoast Digital Press, Inc., in Sarasota, Florida. She offers book services including book development, editing, and publishing. Currently, she is leading a virtual Master Class for people all over the country, who want to write a nonfiction, authority-building book in order to gain instant credibility, secure speaking engagements, and reach a much larger audience. She is the author of *You Should Write A Book!*

Bonnie DeMars is a writer with a focus on memoir. Her pieces appear in online and print publications. She has led a weekly writing group in Alexandria, Virginia, since 2010. Besides writing, Bonnie expresses herself in quilting and gardening. She grew up in Rhode Island and completed a thirty-year Army career as an occupational therapist.

Mary De Vries is retired "at present" but teaches for Hutchinson Community College, works at Hutchinson Middle School 7 as an ELL aide, and does grocery demos at Dillons. She says, "I am still writing. Life is good."

Mary Jo Doig joined Story Circle Network in 2001. While sharing her own life stories, she discovered numerous ways she could support other women with similar goals. She is a past thirteen-year editor for the "True Words from Real Women" section of SCN's quarterly *Journal,* a past ten-year facilitator of writing e-circle 7, and long-time editor for Story Circle Book Reviews. Recently, she has facilitated several lifewriting workshops and Older Women's Legacy (OWL) Workshops in her local Virginia communities, as well as an ongoing lifewriting circle. Mary Jo's stories have been published in *Kitchen Table Stories,* edited by M. Jane Ross, in SCN annual anthologies, in varied periodicals, and in LaJoie magazine. Her blog is *Musings from a Patchwork Quilt Life.* Her memoir, *Stitching a Patchwork Life,* is scheduled for publication in the autumn of 2018. maryjod.wordpress.com

Debra Dolan is an avid reader of women's memoir, and a private journal writer for many, many years. She lives on the west coast of Canada. While slowly healing from a head injury, her internal creative life is expanding in unexpected ways as she reviews the chronicles of her life's journey dating back to 1969.

Bea Epstein is a writer and psychotherapist, living in Rockville, Maryland. Seventeen of her stories have been published in literary journals and magazines, such as *The Connecticut Review, Potomac Review, The Storyteller, Rosebud, Poetica,* and *Passager.* In 2015, a collection of Bea's stories, *Crossing the Bridge,* a memoir of childhood experiences as the daughter of immigrant parents from Eastern Europe, was published. One of her stories was selected as a finalist for the Brooklyn Nonfiction Literary Prize, 2013. Her work was awarded Honorable Mention in the National League of American Pen Women Literary Competition, 2012.

Shawn Essed lives in Maryland with her husband and 3 children. She loves to garden, teach yoga, and take long walks in beautiful places.

Sara Etgen-Baker's love for words began when, as a young girl, her mother read the dictionary to her every night. A teacher's unexpected whisper, "You've got writing talent," ignited her writing desire. Although Sara ignored that whisper and pursued a different career, she eventually rediscovered her inner writer and began writing memoir vignettes and personal narratives. Some of her work has been published in anthologies and magazines, including *Chicken Soup for the Soul,* Guideposts, My Heroic Journey, The Santa Claus Project, Wisdom has a Voice, Finding Mr. Right, and *Times They Were A Changing: Women Remember the 60s & 70s.* She's currently writing her first novel, *Dillehay Crossing.* When not writing, Sara enjoys spending time with her husband Bill.

Susan Flemr is fully retired after a career in nursing and ministry. She and her husband have returned to Iowa, where much of their married life has been spent. Susan delights in her cello playing, reading voraciously, and writing. Life is precious and joy-filled as she keeps up with the activities of her children and grandchildren around Iowa and in Colorado.

Bonnie Frazier lives on the southern Oregon coast with her recently retired husband, autistic son, and two cats. A retired teacher, she spends her days puttering in the garden, cooking, crocheting, and reading. One of her passions is singing and listening to Southern Gospel music. She plays guitar and attended a singing school in Nashville to study music theory and shape-note singing. Another passion is kayaking. Bonnie has trouble passing by any body of water without wishing she was paddling on it. Besides her husband and son, she has two other adult children, two granddaughters, and one granddog.

Mary Lee Fulkerson is a former professional basket artist, who once told stories around her baskets. When her hands rebelled, she began telling stories in a different way—by writing them down. A fourth generation Nevadan and graduate of the University of Nevada - Reno, she is author of *Weavers of Tradition and Beauty: Basketmakers of the Great Basin*, as well as *A Basket of Blessings*, a perpetual calendar. Her newest book, *Women Artists of the Great Basin*, was partly inspired by WSCN storytellers. Outside of her wonderful family and the Nevada outback, memoir is her great love.

In 2013, **Connie Lynn Gray** was a finalist in the nonfiction division of the Texas Writers League Manuscript Contest. She says, "Unfortunately, that was also the year I became active in politics.

The past four years of my life have been devoted to the nonprofit I founded, TexasAdopteeRights.org and I will soon step down as president."

Jeanne Guy is an author, speaker, seasoned facilitator, and reflective writing coach. She is co-author of *Seeing Me: a guide to reframing the way you see yourself through reflective writing*. With dry wit, vulnerability, and an encouraging facilitation style, Jeanne offers personal growth-through-writing workshops and retreats, and blogs (almost) monthly. She is completing a memoir, *You'll Never Find Us*, the story of how her children were stolen from her and how she stole them back. You should pre-order the book. Her three kids are grown now, with kids and dogs of their own. She and her architect husband Robert live in it's-hot-here-Austin, with a couple of ornery cats. http://www.jeanne-guy.com

P. Jan Hall describes herself as "a relocated South Dakotan by way of New Mexico, now living in Oklahoma. I'm only 16 weeks away from completing an MS in Addiction Counseling. I work at Rose State College as a tutor and an Adjunct Professor teaching Creative Writing. I facilitate an OWL Circle and a Story Circle, and wouldn't give either up for anything. I love helping women realize how important their personal stories are, and I love helping them bring their stories to life. I can think of no greater honor than to help my sisters find words for their thoughts, feelings, and memories."

Linda M. Hasselstrom's writing—seventeen books in print—reflects more than fifty years of ranching with concern for the grasslands. Her ranch hosts the Great Plains Native Plant Society's botanic garden for arid grasslands plants. She is the full-time resident writer at her Windbreak House Writing Retreats, and has served as an online mentor for the University of Minnesota's Split Rock writing program, as visiting faculty at Iowa State University - Ames, and advisor to Texas Tech University Press. Linda's most recent books are *Gathering the Grasslands: A Plains Journal* and *Dakota: Bones, Grass, Sky, Collected and New Poems*. Her website and Facebook page provide details about her writing and her writing retreat. Read her blog at WindbreakHouse.wordpress.com. More at www.windbreakhouse.com

Sandra K. Heggen is a retired medical technologist living in Central Texas with her life partner of nearly forty years, as well as a Catahoula-mix dog and an Anatolian Shepherd, both rescued strays. Sam has had to cut back on her writing due to medical and physical issues for both her and her partner. Thus, she says, "the news that this piece was chosen for inclusion in *Inside and Out* is a welcome reminder that there is still hope."

Kim Heikkila, PhD, is an oral historian and former adjunct professor of history. Her first book, *Sisterhood of War: Minnesota Women in Vietnam*, was a finalist for a 2012 Minnesota Book Award. Her creative nonfiction has been published in Broad!, The Grief Diaries, Under the Gum Tree, and elsewhere. She launched her consulting business, Spotlight Oral History, in 2016. Her current writing project blends history and family memoir in its focus on her mother's experience as an "unwed mother" who delivered, and surrendered for adoption, a baby girl (Kim's half-sister) at the Salvation Army's Booth Memorial Hospital in St. Paul in 1961. Kim is also a boxing coach and program director for Rock Steady Boxing Minneapolis at Uppercut Gym.

Kira Janene Holt lives and writes from the top of a hill outside of Austin, Texas. After thirty+ years in education, she retired to focus on writing. Kira writes fiction, creative nonfiction, and self-help materials to assist parents and students in making the transition from secondary to postsecondary education. Her passion is to help with college planning—including entrance exams, financial aid, scholarships, essay writing, college searches, and applications. Kira's currently published fiction is *Rapid Descent – Nightmare in the Grand Canyon*. She's writing the sequel, *Fantasy Rocked Reality*, as well as other fiction and memoir. She blogs at www.kiraholt.com about her "Struggles with Life After 50" and her creative writing projects.

Linda Hoye is the author of *Two Hearts: An Adoptee's Journey Through Grief to Gratitude*. She lives in British Columbia with her husband and their doted-upon Yorkshire terrier, where she gardens in the summer and hibernates in the winter. Retired from a twenty-five-year corporate career in Information Technology and Human Resource Management Systems, she spends her days pursuing creativity through writing, photography, and growing vegetables. She wrangles words and posts photographs daily at A Slice of Life. www.lindahoye.com

Laura Strathman Hulka has been writing all her life, following the path of her mother and sister, both of whom wrote for small publications and groups. She is a third-generation feminist, having grown up on the stories of her grandmother's marching for the 19th Amendment. Laura has always lived in rural environments, including a nine-year stint in Tennessee, learning to speak Southern. She has recently returned to college for her BA in Women's Studies. She lives in Grass Valley, California, in the Sierra foothills. She has been married for 43 years, and has two grown children, 35 and 37.

Kathi Kouguell is a writer and visual artist, who combines the powerful use of words, colors, and design into an emotional and meaningful experience. Her writing always takes her to past events, thoughts, feelings of joy and sadness. The work then leads to large installations, wooden structures, framed pieces, or large hand-painted and quilted hangings. Each piece is a strong combination of words, story, feelings and emotions, colors, design, and textures. SCN's March 2010 Journal included her piece "Requiem."

After living nearly a decade in Yemen, **Khadijah Lacina** and her family have settled on a permaculture-based homestead in the Missouri Ozarks. She is a writer, translator, teacher, herbalist, and fiber artist.

Pat LaPointe is a past President of the Story Circle Network and is currently editor of the *Changes In Life* monthly newsletter for women. She facilitates women's writing groups online and on-site. Her anthology of women's stories, *The Woman I've Become: 37 Women Share Their Journey from Toxic Relationships to Self-Empowerment*, was published in 2012. She shares her Prospect Heights, Illinois, home with her husband and a spirited Yorkie.

Juniper Lauren is a writer, environmental engineer, and rough-water kayaker. She lives and writes from a place where deep wilderness meets urban political engagement. She is a founder of Undoing Racism Austin and a member of the Story Circle community of women writers. Her work has been published in several anthologies and magazines, including Sea Kayaker Magazine. When not at her desk, you are likely to find

Juniper scouting the Lake Austin shore for ripe wild cherries. Or find her at her website: WildShoreJourneys.com.

Maya Lazarus enjoyed teaching English to non-native speakers, both children and adults, for 22 years in Colombia, Costa Rica, and in upstate New York. When she wanted to change careers, she became a development editor of educational materials. Now retired, she enjoys journal writing, flash fiction, nonfiction, haiku poetry, and is working on a memoir (almost complete). Several short pieces and poems have been published in the Story Circle Journal as well as a flash fiction piece in flashfictionmagazine online. Maya moved to central Texas from the East Coast in 2014, and lives on five acres with her husband and four dogs.

Helen (Len) Leatherwood, Program Coordinator for SCN's Online Classes program, has been teaching writing privately to students in Beverly Hills for the past 17 years. She has received regional and national teacher awards for the past 7 years from the Scholastic Artists and Writers Awards, the oldest and most prestigious writing contest for youth in the US. She is a daily blogger at 20 Minutes a Day, as well as a published writer of flash fiction and memoir, with pieces appearing in flashquake, longstoryshort, All Things Girl, SCN's True Words Anthology, Provo Canyon Review, as well as *A Cup of Comfort Cookbook*. She was a 2015 nominee for a Pushcart Prize, the best of the small presses.

Tucson writer **Ethel Lee-Miller** continues her love affair...with words, adding storyteller to her list of "wordplay," along with life skills, writing process, public speaking presentations, memoir, personal essay, and short stories. Published works includes her memoir *Thinking of Miller Place*, a twin's family perspective, and *Seedlings, Stories of Relationships*, some true, some "enhanced." Ethel's work has been accepted for *Muse Matrix*, a women's anthology of writing and art; SCN's Real Women Write Anthology 2016; and online journals. Improvisation classes make up her latest adventure with words. "Every event, no matter how mundane or crazy, offers delicious seeds for my gardens of stories." She blogs about the writing life at http://etheleemiller.com

Karen Wampold Levine turned 80 in May of 2017. She says, "My three sons, their wives, and my four grandsons, though scattered about the country, keep in close touch. We talk (almost) every Sunday. They always remember to send birthday and Mother's Day cards and lots of interesting and beautiful photographs that they've taken near their homes and on trips. I gaze at these masterpieces frequently and show my friends every chance I get. My activities now consist of lunch groups, book club, senior yoga classes, and walks in the neighborhood with a friend and her wonderful black Pomeranian dog. What a glorious life I lead."

Juliana Lightle was raised on a family farm in Northwestern Missouri, and became a college administrator, corporate manager, racehorse breeder, management consultant, educator, and author. She holds a PhD in counseling and business from The Ohio State University and two degrees from the University of Rhode Island. She currently teaches high school, sings, raises horses, and writes from a canyon rim in the Panhandle of Texas. Her latest book, *On the Rim of Wonder*, a memoir in poems, was published in 2014.

Susan Lines lives on Gabriola Island, a small isle just off Vancouver Island, British Columbia. "I am the proud mother of two beautiful young women, and granny to six gorgeous healthy

grandchildren, three of whom are triplets—they are the youngest at 17 yrs. I am also very lucky to have reconnected with my
soul mate. Together we have four wonderful young adults, and
seven grandchildren. All of whom are happy and healthy. I love
to paint, write, and listen to good music. Gardening, reading,
and animals are other passions."

Rose McCorkle is a retired educator, living in Austin, Texas, with
her wife and their teenaged niece. Between taking care of her family, Rose occasionally finds time to read, tend a plethora of or-
chids, and volunteer for NAMI, the National Alliance on Mental
Illness. Most importantly, she loves spending time with her two
wonderful grandchildren, as they fill her with joy and delight.

Sheila McNaughton is a Realtor, writer, and assemblage artist.
Having completed her mystery novel, *You Don't Know What
I Have Done*, she is searching for a literary agent. Involved in
the local writing community for many years, Sheila facilitated
the creative writing Story Circle meeting for seven years and
the Florida Writers Association St Petersburg Chapter for three
years. She has written a book on holiday decorations and is
working on a children's story, *The Fairy Garden*.

Judy M. Miller is a parent educator and coach focusing on adoption. She parents four kiddos with her husband—three through
adoption. Judy is the author of *What to Expect From Your Adopted
Tween* and *Writing to Heal Adoption Grief: Making Connections
& Moving Forward*. Her expertise is frequently quoted by outlets such as TODAY.com, and in publications such as Parenting, and The Open-Hearted Way to Open Adoption. Her articles
and essays are carried throughout North America in parenting
magazines and well-known anthologies, like *Chicken Soup for the*

Soul. Judy directed and produced the 2013, 2014, and 2015 seasons of "Listen To Your Mother Indianapolis." She is currently taking a break from nonfiction writing, venturing into romance under a pen name.

Merimée Moffitt is a California ex-pat who's lived in New Mexico since 1970. A complete bio appears in her recent memoir (reviewed by Story Circle Book Reviews): *Free Love, Free Fall: Scenes from the West Coast Sixties.* She has an MA from the University of New Mexico in English/Creative Writing. Her poems have been widely published, most recently in Persimmon Tree, an online literary review for older women. Her latest book of poems (co-authored with Georgia Santa Maria) is called *Berlin Poems and Photographs.* Merimée taught in secondary school and community college. She lives with her husband and dog, and hopes to soon finish her fourth book about addiction in the family. She has a blended family of four kids and four grandkids. Find her at merimeemoffitt.wordpress.com

Sallie Moffitt is an award-winning author whose work has been anthologized in SCN's *True Words*, and published in literary journals such as "Ten Spurs." She has worked as an editor and a writing contest judge. She is active in the self-help community and regularly shares her story, so others can see that hope is available even in the darkest circumstances.

Sally Nielsen is a retired college English and Literature teacher living on Florida's northeastern coast. Recent publications include "The Bootleg Daughter" in Persimmon Tree, in its September 2011 online issue. "The Baptism Years" received an honorable mention from Glimmer Train Magazine's Family Matters contest, in December 2011. Sally contributed a piece about losing her hair to chemotherapy, appearing in "Readers Write" for The Sun Magazine in June 2017. A meditator and Christian meditation teacher, she gives workshops to interested non-writers on lifewriting topics, such as how to write an ethical will, spiritual autobiography, and finding your own life story. She is writing a memoir, *The Land Between Us*, about growing up on and being the last inheritor of Midwestern farm-family land, 151 years in the family, and then … giving it up.

Retired from teaching high school for many years, **Lucy Painter** began writing down many of the family stories she heard growing up in western Virginia, stories she found universal after her many travels around the US and Europe. She lives in Williamsburg, Virginia, with her husband of 49 years, two Dachshunds, and one very old cat. Lucy has been an active member of Story Circle Network for eight years.

Mary Ann Parker has made homes in many places but has been rooted for the past 25 years in Texas. She and her husband live on the Gulf Coast, sharing their home with the youngest of their three sons, and his family. "I participate in a poetry group begun with church friends. Other joys are music, old rose and herb gardening, adventuring with (six) grandchildren, and writing weekly for three blogs." In 2010, Mary Ann self-published a collection of photos called *Eyes of the Heart*, as well as a blog-to-book collection of poetry and short essays titled *Stones and Feathers, a different way of seeing*. She published a 2012 Christmas collection titled *Standing on Tiptoe, Reaching for the Light*. And a piece from her "Kitchen Keepers" blog was chosen in 2013 to be in *Roots, Where Food Comes From and Where it Takes Us*, a BlogHer Anthology.

An Austin resident since the late 1960s, **Jane Louise Steig Parsons** has worn a variety of hats: child, elementary-high school-graduate student, and bassoonist (Palo Alto), research educational psychologist (UT), artist, poet, writer, dancer, professional photographer, wife, mother, grandmother, and appreciative Story Circle Network member (Austin). Her writing and photographs have appeared in numerous publications and exhibits.

Teri Heard Ralbovsky is a writer living in Chelmsford, Massachusetts, with her husband Peter, her 13-year-old son PJ, and their beagle Max. Through her writing, Teri explores her journey to motherhood as well as the daily balancing of family life, writing, and career. Examples of some of her musings can be read at https://teriheardralbovsky.blogspot.com. In addition to writing, Teri loves to read, hike, cook, bike, and canoe, as well spend time at the beach and in the mountains.

Born in pre-independence India, **Sipra Roy** devoted her life to teaching underprivileged children, helping them to graduate high school. After retiring, she moved to New York City to be near her children, and continues a passion for writing poetry, memoir, and on social issues. She also enjoys New York's cultural diversity.

Andrea Savee lives in Lakewood, California. Her work has appeared in many literary journals, anthologies, and blogs. View her video version of "Waking" on YouTube. See more of her work with words and images at https://onewomansday.wordpress.com/category/andrea-savee/

As a certified Life Legacy facilitator, personal historian, and memoir mentor, **Susanna Schuerman** helps people to discover and record their life stories. Through reflective, contemplative writing, she encourages writers to deepen their relationship with the spiritual and natural world. Sue's writings have appeared in various anthologies and other publications. Her award-winning "Following the Road to Lindi" was published in the Story Circle Journal in September 2016. Now that Sue is retired, she is recalibrating her time to lead workshops, complete her own memoir, and encourage other writers to develop their craft. She is a co-director of the annual Christian Writers Workshop and leads the local monthly Cedar Falls Christian Writers Group.

Cathy Marie Scibelli is retired freelance writer. She now maintains a Facebook page with her sidekick Stretch Bear, writing words of encouragement for her friends and others going through tough times. Cathy herself has been fighting Metastatic Breast Cancer for several years.

Johnett Scogin is recently retired and lives in Austin with her wife, Rose, a teenage niece, and multiple fur children. She feels like the most lucky woman on earth—she's become a grandmother to two children without ever having children of her own. "Awesome!"

Former journalist **Sandra Shackelford**, a professional artist, writing instructor, and oral historian, has facilitated Women's Writing Circles in Green Bay, Wisconsin, for the past decade. Her poetry has appeared in *IMAGE*, an anthology of poetry published in 2014. In 2015, Ms. Shackelford and members of her writing circles published *Word for Word*, an anthology of nonfiction and poetry. She presented a writing workshop at Green Bay's Untitled Town Book Festival in the spring of 2017. Sandra is currently at work on her memoir, which chronicles the eleven years she spent dedicated to fighting for equality and social justice at St. Francis Information Center, Greenwood, Mississippi.

Mid-life, **Connie Spittler** changed lanes, from writer/produc-er of film and video to writer of literary essays, short stories, and poetry. After her work appeared in twenty anthologies, she moved on to publish a novel, book of poetry, creative nonfiction, and two illustrated nature essay books, one a Southwest Book of the Year, the other, the winner in the National League of Amer-ican Pen Women (NLAPW) Biennial Competition. Her latest book, a women's fiction/mystery titled *The Erotica Book Club for Nice Ladies*, won one national and two international awards. While living in Tucson, the University of Arizona Writing Works Center invited her to teach workshops focused on women telling their stories, still one of her favorite things to encourage. She now lives in Omaha, Nebraska.

Amber Lea Starfire is an author, editor, and creative writing coach, whose passion is helping others tell their stories. Her most recent books include *Not the Mother I Remember: A Memoir* (ex-cerpted here)—a finalist for both the 2015 Next Generation In-die Book Awards and the 2013-2014 Sarton Women's Literary Awards—and *Week by Week: A Year's Worth of Journaling Prompts & Meditations*. Amber is also co-editor of the award-winning anthology, *Times They Were A-Changing: Women Remember the '60s & '70s*. Her creative nonfiction and poetry have appeared in numerous anthologies and literary journals.

Penelope Starr is a writer, founder and producer of Odyssey Storytelling, Executive Director of StoryArts Group, Inc., workshop presenter, community activist, citizen folklorist, and restorer of Navajo rugs. She is the author of *The Radical Act of Community Storytelling: Empowering Voices in Uncensored Events* (2017). Her new passions are consulting with commu-nities to begin their own storytelling events and finishing her novel built of linked short stories. See more at www.Penelope-Starr.com.

Margaret Stephenson is a social worker, an artist, and a journaler living in the hills of Austin, Texas. She home schools her youngest child while helping her two older kids navigate young adulthood. Trusting her children to pave their own way sparked the realization that she could do the same for herself. She earned her black belt in Kung Fu, studied Tai Chi, renewed her social work license, learned to draw, began drinking coffee, started eating meat, painted her house in bright colors, and weathered the ups and downs of family life without too much emotional drama. Her oldest child, Kaley, who pushed for home schooling, is now twenty. She is a sign language interpreter, a writer, a musician, and a passionate explorer of life.

Janice Strohmeier is originally form Calgary, Alberta. After earning her MA in History at Sam Houston State, and taking out US citizenship in 2007, Janice became a history professor with Lone Star College in Houston. She is also involved in Adult Education teaching high school to adults in the GED program. In her spare time, Janice studies piano, likes to exercise, and to putter in her garden. She lives with her husband of twenty-two years, Paul, and their three Boxers: Mercy, Isaac, and Jones. They also work with Lone Star Boxer Rescue, taking in foster-Boxers who are waiting for their forever homes. Lots of belly-rubs, toy-tugs, and sloppy kisses on a daily basis in their home. A regular contributor to SCN and an e-circle facilitator, Janice only writes when she is breathing.

Lanie Tankard is a freelance editor, writer, researcher, and reviewer in Austin. A former production editor of Contemporary

Psychology: A Journal of Reviews, she has been an editorial writer for the Florida Times-Union in Jacksonville and a creative writer for Lewis Advertising Agency in Mobile, Alabama. She also taught writing at Texas State University as well as English as a Second Language in Ngaremlengui State (Republic of Palau, Western Caroline Islands, Oceania). She has a Bachelor's in journalism from the University of Florida (Gainesville) and an MA in journalism from the University of Texas (Austin). Tankard belongs to the National Book Critics Circle and the Society for Scholarly Publishing. https://lanietankard.wordpress.com

Marian McCaa Thomas is a semi-retired church musician who teaches piano and harpsichord, enjoys reading, gardening, volunteering at her church, and spending time with friends. She also keeps tabs on her three grown children, two granddaughters, and husband of 54 years. Her grandchildren live in the same college town where her included story took place. Marian is writing a biography of her mother, who lived from 1911 to 2011, and whose weekly letters, treasured and saved through the years, are providing insights into how her mother turned seeming obstacles into opportunities throughout her life.

Susan J. Tweit is a botanist who began her career studying wildfires, grizzly bear habitat, and sagebrush communities, before turning to writing as a way to celebrate the nature of life, human and wild. She has written twelve books, including the memoir *Walking Nature Home*, hailed as a "must read." Tweit's work has won awards including the Colorado Book Award, the EDDIE for magazine writing, and ForeWord's Book of the Year. Her stories and essays have appeared in magazines and newspapers ranging from *Audubon* and *Popular Mechanics* to *High Country News* and the *Los Angeles Times*. She is a columnist for *Rocky Mountain Gar-*

dening magazine and Houzz.com, and spends her free time restoring nature in Yellowstone National Park.

Cameo Victor – Deceased.

Jo Virgil recently retired from a career in journalism (newspaper and magazine freelance writing) and community relations with Barnes & Noble and then the Texas Governor's Office. She has a Master of Journalism degree with a minor in Environmental Science, reflecting her love of writing and appreciation of nature. She always carries with her the words of one of her journalism professors: "Stories are what make us matter." Jo has been a Story Circle Network member for many years, is editor of "True Words" for the SCN Journal, and is a participant in the SCN WordWeavers group in Austin.

Jude Walsh is a proud Story Circle Past President and Board member. She writes memoir, personal essay, poetry, and fiction. She's published at Mothers Always Write, Literary Mama, The ManifestStation, Flights Magazine, Indiana Voices Journal, and the SCN quarterly Journal. Her work is also in numerous anthologies including *True Words from Real Women, The AWW Scholarship Collection* (2014, 2015, 2016), *The Anthology of Tragedies and Triumphs,* and *Kitchen Table Stories.* Her craft essay won third place and publication in *The Magic of Memoir: Inspiration for the Writing Journey* (2016). In 2017 her essay, Bonus Pay, was featured in *Chicken Soup For the Soul: Inspiration for Teachers.* Jude shares her Dayton, Ohio, home with her son and three dogs, but no cat!

Judy Sheer Watters, retired English teacher and secondary principal, leads Hill Country Legacy Writers and Hill Country Christian Writers. She is a freelance writer, editor, and co-owner of Franklin Scribes Publishers. Author of *The Road Home: The*

Legacy that was, is, and is to Come (2013), and *How to Hitch-hike from Texas to California in 3 Days in 14 Easy Steps* (2017), Judy has also contributed to several anthologies, magazines, and newspapers. Her greatest joy is helping others find their own voice to write their stories for their families and for the generations to come. She and her husband live in Spring Branch, Texas, and enjoy spending time with their three adult children, one daughter-in-law, and two grandcats.

Susan G. Weidener is an author and former staff writer with "The Philadelphia Inquirer." She has written two memoirs, *Again in a Heartbeat: a memoir of love, loss and dating again*, and its sequel, *Morning at Wellington Square*. Her novel, *A Portrait of Love and Honor*, is based on a true story. Susan grew up in Wayne, Pennsylvania, attended American University in Washington, DC, and received her Master's degree in education from the University of Pennsylvania. She teaches memoir and fiction to adults, and facilitates the Women's Writing Circle, a support and critique group for writers in suburban Philadelphia. Susan lives with her Yellow Lab, Lily, in Chester Springs, Pennsylvania. Her website is: http://www.susanweidener.com/

Rhonda Wiley-Jones self-published her coming-of-age travel memoir, *At Home in the World: Travel Stories of Growing Up and Growing Away*, in 2014. She is a professional speaker and workshop facilitator. She is currently writing an historical adventure fiction, *Salwar Kameeze*, in which an unconventional young woman in 1906 sails alone to India to sell her uncle's horses and discovers turbulent waters aboard ship and in India. Two men and a mentor help salvage her misguided self-identity. Rhonda's short stories, essays, and travel memoirs are published on the WritingIt-Real website and in anthologies, such as *Saturday Writers' Tenth*

Anniversary Edition; God Still Speaks; Love Is in the Air; True Words from Real Women; and poetry in *Ethos*. Visit Rhonda's website and blog at: http://FindingOurselvesAtHomeintheWorld.com.

Susan C. Williams – Information unavailable.

Linda C. Wisniewski is a former librarian who shares an empty nest with her retired scientist husband in Bucks County, Pennsylvania, where she writes for a weekly newspaper, teaches memoir workshops, and speaks on the healing power of writing. Her work has been published in literary magazines and anthologies. She has won fiction and essay contests from the Wild River Review, the Pearl S. Buck Writing Center, and Mom Writers Literary Magazine, and was nominated for a Pushcart Prize. Linda's memoir, *Off Kilter: A Woman's Journey to Peace with Scoliosis, Her Mother and Her Polish Heritage* was published by Pearlsong Press. Her unpublished novel, *Where the Stork Flies*, was a finalist for the 2015 Eludia Award.

Carol Ziel describes herself as "a 69-year-old woman who has had been writing since fourth grade. My life has been frequently chaotic, traumatic, and occasionally adventurous. I'm honored to share parts of the journey. I'm a social worker by trade, gardener by passion, a Quaker and Goddess-centered woman who has come to a place of peace."

About the Editors

Susan F. Schoch, editor, is a freelance writer and editor in Colorado, specializing in personal history. Her most recent book is *The Clay Connection,* a study of ceramic artists Jim and Nan McKinnell, for the American Museum of Ceramic Art. She reviews writing by and about women at Story Circle Book Reviews and is the editor of the quarterly SCN Journal and the annual SCN Anthology, *Real Women Write: Sharing Our Stories, Sharing Our Lives.*

Susan Wittig Albert, editorial board member, is the author of memoirs, mysteries, historical fiction, and nonfiction. She has been published by several traditional publishers and also publishes her work under her own imprint, Persevero Press. Susan founded SCN in 1997 and is currently (2015-2017) serving as its president. She and her husband Bill live in the Texas Hill Country.

Mary Jo Doig, editorial board member, joined Story Circle Network in 2001. She is a past editor for "True Words" in SCN's quarterly Journal, a past facilitator of writing e-circle 7, and a long-time editor for Story Circle Book Reviews. She has facilitated several lifewriting workshops and Older Women's Legacy (OWL) Workshops. Mary Jo's stories have been published in *Kitchen Table Stories,* in SCN annual anthologies, and in varied periodicals including LaJoie magazine. Her blog is Musings from a Patchwork Quilt Life. Her memoir, *Stitching a Patchwork Life,* is scheduled for publication in the autumn of 2018.

Pat LaPointe, editorial board member, is a past President of the Story Circle Network and is currently editor of the *Changes In Life* monthly newsletter for women. She facilitates women's writing groups online and on-site. Her anthology of women's stories, *The Woman I've Become: 37 Women Share Their Journey from Toxic Relationships to Self-Empowerment,* was published in 2012. She shares her Prospect Heights, Illinois, home with her husband and a spirited Yorkie.

Jo Virgil, editorial board member, recently retired from a career in journalism (newspaper and magazine freelance writing) as well as community relations with Barnes & Noble and then the Texas Governor's Office. She has a Master of Journalism degree with a minor in Environmental Science, reflecting her love of writing and appreciation of nature. She always carries with her the words of one of her journalism professors: "Stories are what make us matter." Jo has been a Story Circle Network member for many years, is editor of "True Words" for the SCN Journal, and is a participant in the SCN WordWeavers group in Austin.

Jude Walsh, editorial board member, is a Story Circle Past President and Board member. She writes memoir, personal essay, poetry, and fiction, appearing in Mothers Always Write, Literary Mama, The ManifestStation, Flights Magazine, Indiana Voices Journal, and the SCN Journal. Her work is anthologized in *True Words from Real Women, The AWW Scholarship Collection* (2014, 2015, 2016), *The Anthology of Tragedies and Triumphs,* and *Kitchen Table Stories.* Her craft essay won third place and publication in *The Magic of Memoir: Inspiration for the Writing Journey* (2016). In 2017 her essay, Bonus Pay, was featured in *Chicken Soup For the Soul: Inspiration for Teachers.* Jude shares her Dayton, Ohio, home with her son and three dogs, but no cat!

ABOUT STORY CIRCLE NETWORK: FOR WOMEN WITH STORIES TO TELL

by Susan Wittig Albert

We learn best to listen to our own voices if we are listening at the same timeto other women, whose stories, for all our differences, turn out, if we listen well,to be our stories also.
— Barbara Deming

I'm going to use the personal pronoun when I tell you about SCN, because I am its founder and a current member of this wonderful organization. I am very proud of—and often amazed by—all we have done and continue to do.

Chartered in 1997 as a nonprofit organization, SCN is now twenty years old and still growing. Over the years, nearly 4,000 women in this country and elsewhere in the world have been members, and many times that number have participated in our programs. Our activities are funded by annual membership dues and fee-based programs, as well as the generous gifts and grants of friends and supporters. Our work is done by a very small paid staff and dozens of volunteers.

Story Circle Network is dedicated to helping women share the stories of their lives and to raising public awareness of the importance of women's personal histories. We carry out our mission through publications, websites, award programs, online and face-to-face classes and workshops, writing and reading circles, blogs, and many woman-focused activities. We sponsor a biannual national women's writing conference, weekend writing retreats called "LifeLines," and a regular program of online classes.

We sponsor Story Circle Book Reviews, the largest and oldest women's book review site on the Internet, and the annual Sarton Women's Writing Awards.

We encourage our members to publish their writing through our quarterly *Story Circle Journal*, annual *Anthology*, and blogs ("Herstories" and "One Woman's Day"). In addition, SCN has published three anthologies of members' and others' writing: *With Courage and Common Sense: Memoirs from the Older Women's Legacy Circle*, *What Wildness is This: Women Write about the Southwest*, *Kitchen Table Stories*—and now, *Inside and Out*.

But what I have just told you about what we are doing at SCN today is likely to be out of date tomorrow, for we continue to explore new ways to serve the growing community of women writers and those who are interested in documenting and celebrating women's lives.

So I invite you to visit our central website, www.storycircle. org, and from there, explore the many activities SCN has created to support women with stories to tell. We're here to help, because we believe in women's stories. Please join us.

BOOKS PUBLISHED BY STORY CIRCLE NETWORK

Inside and Out: Women's Truths, Women's Stories
edited by Susan F. Schoch

Kitchen Table Stories
edited by Jane Ross

Starting Points
by Susan Wittig Albert

What Wildness Is This: Women Write About the Southwest
edited by Susan Wittig Albert, Susan Hanson,
Jan Epton Seale, Paula Stallings Yost

With Courage and Common Sense:
Memoirs from the Older Women's Legacy Circle
edited by Susan Wittig Albert and Dayna Finet

Writing From Life
by Susan Wittig Albert

ANTHOLOGIES

True Words from Real Women, the SCN Anthology, 2009-2010
edited by Amber Lea Starfire

True Words from Real Women, the SCN Anthology, 2011-2013
edited by Mary Jo Doig

True Words from Real Women, the SCN Anthology, 2014
edited by Susan F. Schoch

Real Women Write, the SCN Anthology, 2015-2017
edited by Susan F. Schoch

81200498R00150

Made in the USA
Lexington, KY
13 February 2018